VALERIE
THE WHIRLWIND

Valerie

The Whirlwind

My Life & Adventures

I hope that you enjoy the read. Valerie August. 2021.

Valerie Young OStJ RGN RMN CPN
cert Dip HE Retd.

Bound Biographies

Copyright Valerie Young © 2021

Produced in association with

Bound Biographies

10 Pipits Croft, Bicester, OX26 6XW

www.boundbiographies.com

ISBN: 978-1-905178-86-5

Typeset in Garamond by www.wordsbydesign.co.uk

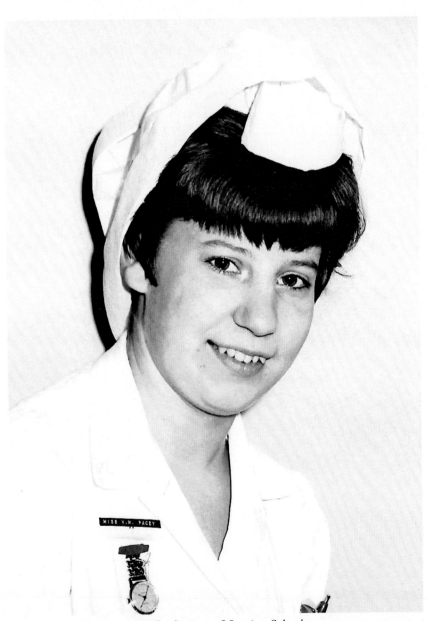

At Preliminary Nursing School

DEDICATION

This book is dedicated firstly to my parents who brought me up to believe I could achieve anything that I wanted with hard work; to my two husbands for putting up with me and wanting them to help me with many jobs and projects; to my two sons for their love and companionship over the years, and for my adopted daughter Linda, whose perseverance makes me so proud of her.

ACKNOWLEDGMENTS

I would like to thank those who have helped and given me support during the lockdown, and being willing to edit my writings, which has enabled me to stay focused. John, my patient, helpful husband, Dot Barber MSc. BA (Hons), RGN, MBACP, my lifelong friend, John Williams KStJ, St John County President, Matthew and Stephen, my sons and Pat Chesterton MBE, former St John County Secretary. I also thank The Bucks Herald for use of some of the photographs.

Contents

FOREWORD

I was both pleased and privileged to be asked to write the Foreword for Valerie's life story. Valerie conceived this a 'Lockdown Project' to fill the time because her travelling wings were well and truly clipped.

Born in the same year as Valerie and being brought up in Wolverton, I found her early descriptions of Bletchley and North Bucks very evocative. I well remember the Co-op coffee bar! Interestingly, I never knew her then, despite being a Wolverton Ambulance Cadet at the same time, but her memories of the Cadet Competitions, Inspections, Camp and the Green Park Leadership weekends are very comprehensive.

Much later on in our St John service I had much more contact and admired her tenacity and desire to take St John into new areas. I smiled when I read that her NHS colleagues knew her as 'Val the Whirlwind' and in St John Ambulance she did have the reputation of going where angels feared to tread! She describes herself as a 'rebel' but one who acted from the best motives.

I also smiled at the various formidable ladies who seemed to be in charge of Stoke Mandeville Hospital during her nurse training; we were not without our counterparts in St John Bucks too!

What an intrepid traveller Valerie turned out to be! Combining travel and volunteering, she brought her special skills to the St John Eye Hospital in the Holy Land, the Leprosy Hospital in Myanmar (Burma), St John and other organisations in the West

Indies, Pakistan and Malaysia. Other highlights nearer to the UK were escorting pilgrims to Lourdes and a visit to Rome.

Valerie's mother was a character in her own right, having worked at Bletchley Park and serving as an organist at various churches, including Soulbury. I did not know that Valerie was a pianist and her book displays her deep Christian faith.

Her book takes us back to a different NHS and St John, when individuals took initiatives to improve the care and services to people, particularly in rural communities.

I thoroughly enjoyed reading this book and hope that you will too.

John Williams KStJ
County President St John Ambulance

INTRODUCTION

"Do not run through life so fast that you forget what it's all about, that you forget not only where you have been, but also where you are going."

In writing this life story, I must admit I think that I lived in the best of times! I am one of the baby-boomers born after the war. Rationing was still in place but it did not concern me as a toddler. The war had finished five years previously and people wanted to make a new life for themselves. Dad was demobbed in 1946; he wanted to get married and settle down. My mother had not met anyone at Bletchley Park so Dad seemed a good catch with his own barber's business. She was used to shop life as her parents had run the greengrocer's shop at Fenny Stratford.

I grew up behind the shop and was always used to people calling in and lots of coming and going. My maternal grandparents took me out in the pram a great deal to give my mother a break and to take me away from the shop environment.

The 1950s were good years as industry was getting going again and lots of new houses were being built. The pop songs of the '50s were cheerful and pop culture was lively. How my friends and I enjoyed the children's songs, 'How much is that doggy in the window?', 'Oh, my Papa, to me he is so wonderful', and 'Que sera sera, whatever will be will be', which we sang constantly. I enjoyed going to school and the experience and routine that it gave me. My cousins were older than me and wore fluorescent Teddy Boy socks, pointed shoes and narrow ties and they had the Teddy Boy hairstyle. Brian, my cousin, came to join Dad as his apprentice and learned the new styles on day release at college, and Dad carried on doing the traditional haircuts. My friends and I loved the 'Swinging Sixties'. My first pop record was the Beatles number, 'I want to hold your hand'. Miniskirts and back-combed hair were all the rage. Coffee bars and teenage culture came into its own. We had pocket money and more freedom to go out and around with our friends.

I was so fortunate to be able to do my nurse training at the end of the 1960s and early 1970s. I was mature enough to leave home at 17. It was still the apprentice system of observe, copy and practise. We were left in charge of wards in our third year of training and on night duty. We gained so much experience of different conditions. The discipline gave us security and order. It was quite easy to try different specialities to see what was most suitable for us. Treatments, drugs and healthcare saw massive improvements.

My children grew up in the late 1970s and '80s. They were able to go off and play with friends for a morning or afternoon without any worries. They could play in the park, join any groups, have plenty of hobbies and go on camps. They grew up without the mobile phone, without their heads being stuck into a screen all day. They learnt to socialise and develop excellent communication skills. Most of my St John organising was done by telephone landline. Bedgrove estate had community spirit where you knew your neighbours and it had a central hub around the shops, pub, churches and park. It had its own schools and many groups.

The world was changing rapidly with new technology, but provided we worked hard, kept our heads down and plodded along, one could keep a job for many years. In nursing there was always plenty of work, and extra shifts or agency work would provide for life's extras. During the 1980s many fast food outlets opened as more women went out to work and wanted a quick meal. Many people did less exercise and put weight on! The popular music deteriorated from a melody that we could sing, to beat music, just constant jungle music.

The 1990s gave me more freedom as the boys got older. We could manage more days out and short breaks at Center Parcs. Improvements to the house and newer cars were bought. On looking back how life has changed since the 1950s, we were so fortunate to have not had our world turned upside down, as the previous two generations had with wars, and we could experience long distance travel that our parents had never dreamed of. People are now glued to the mobile phone and internet. There is less face to face contact and different forms of socialising, and many groups relying on volunteers have folded. Yes, I think that I lived through the best of times!

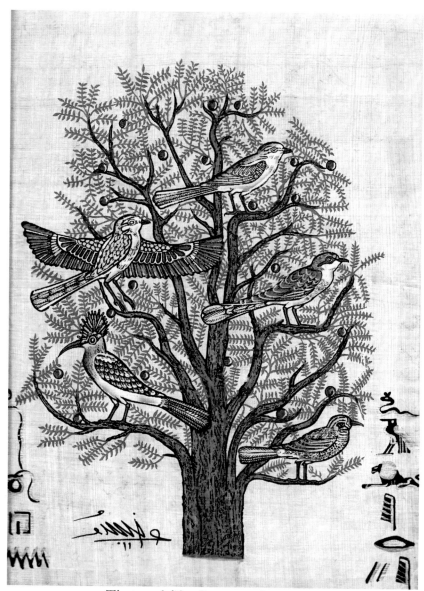

The tree of life - five stages of experience

Part 1

CHAPTER 1
IN THE BEGINNING...

The name Pacey, Pcay, Passey or Paicey, is said to be derived from the Pacy-sur-Eure district of Normandy.

Many such names can be found in Cheshire and they may have come from France during the Norman Conquest. Later, some may have been Huguenots emigrating from France to be free to practise the Protestant religion, as France was a Catholic country and they could be persecuted for their beliefs. Many brought crafts, especially lacemaking, which became prominent at this time.

The Paceys came across to Bletchley from Ridgmont, near Woburn, Bedfordshire. Bruce (my cousin) wonders if they were part of the Paceys from Blisworth, Northamptonshire, in the 1830s. They were shoemakers and lacemakers. It is only twenty miles from Blisworth to Ridgmont. Between 1836-1839, George Pacey and his wife Catherine moved from Ridgmont to Fenny Stratford. They had nine children.

Thomas Pacey, my great grandfather, was born in 1845 and was the middle child. He married Ann Cook and became a master painter and decorator. Thomas and Ann had eight children and I believe that Grandad Pacey (Francis Leonardis) was the eldest. As families were so large in those days, some established plumbing or ironmongery businesses. Some experts say that, more than food and drugs, it was the explosion in piped water installation and better sanitation that improved the nation's health and was the reason for a big drop in the mortality rate from the 1880s. Two cousins (Laurence and Walter) emigrated to America before the First World War seeking their fortunes.

Thomas Pacey, my great grandfather

Our line of the family lived in Park Street, Bletchley. Thomas became a builder and built many houses in Park Street, and even the Halfway House in Bletchley Road, now renamed Captain Ridley's Shooting Party by the Wetherspoon's Group. When he died in 1921, he left £2,540.8s.11d., a tidy sum in those days, to be divided amongst the family. Again, it was the 'bank of Mum and Dad' that lent money to each child to purchase a small terraced house as they got married.

The Pacey Family, circa 1913, at Park Street

Francis Pacey and Sarah Kirby's engagement (my paternal grandparents)

Gert   Nellie   Lou   Sarah

Grampy Kirby   Bertha   Granny

The Kirby family

Grandad Pacey, commonly called Frank, married Sarah Kirby from Bicester. The Kirbys had five daughters and Frank and Sarah had seven children between 1905-1916.

The eldest was Nora, a real character, and then Thomas, the eldest son who was tall and imposing. Next came Ronald, then two years later Beatrice, then Walter and, finally, my father, Reginald who was a twin. His twin, Edgar, only lived for ten days, succumbing to a chest infection. It was survival of the fittest in those days. Dad was nicknamed 'Bawler,' as he was always crying for attention. Sarah, worn out with child rearing and housework, hadn't got much time for the last child, so Nora and Beat played a large part in his care. They told the tale of when he was small and they were knitting... they would ask him to go and find the dropped stitch!

The four Pacey boys

Grandad Pacey was an engine driver at Bletchley Station and would have worked his way up from being a fireman. Long days on the footplate were tiring and he would come home filthy. Grandad Pacey was a big supporter of Bletchley Football Club, serving on their committee in later years. The two girls, Nora and Beat, enjoyed dancing in the 1920s and '30s. They each had a son late in life, with Nora requiring a caesarean birth in 1946. This was before the National Health Service and she would have died without the caesarean, as she was quite a small lady. Both girls were very handy needlewomen and always made us aprons and peg bags for Christmas. Nora also did upholstery work to make ends meet when her husband became incapacitated from lung disease arising from his First World War Army service.

Dad was in the Boys Brigade in his teens and became an accomplished bugler at the Baptist Church. We also have a photograph of him in a school production of 'The Rajah of Rajapore' with his brother Ron.

Francis Pacey, engine driver

Bletchley Post Office and Station

Nora was one for telling family tales. She said how one of the cousins married a man who abused her and drank all the money. He would hit her in a drunken brawl and pull her along by her hair. Nora and the family would often visit and take a basket of food for the poor woman and her children. Another tale was, as a little girl playing in the street, some of the children would shout to them to say that the Duke of Bedford's chauffeur-driven car was going along Bletchley Road on its way to the railway station. All the kids would run along Park Street to see it going to Bletchley Station. This was around 1913 before the First World War.

During the Second World War, Auntie Nora had two children billeted on them from the East End of London. They came in rags and Auntie Nora cleaned them up and gave them fresh clothes. After a while they got homesick and went back to see their family in London. When they returned, they were in rags again and had fleas and nits. Auntie Nora went to see the billeting officer and they were moved and she ended up with two adults who worked at Bletchley Park, which suited her well.

Tom was too old to serve in the Second World War so worked on the ambulances. Ron, again, was in the higher age bracket and went to Bristol to help with aeroplane manufacturing. He eventually settled with his wife and two children in Bridgwater. Uncle Wal loved his tennis and played in many county tournaments. He was called up and went into the Army and was one of the thousands rescued from Dunkirk who lived to tell the tale another day! Wal married Queenie during the war and they had one child, a daughter Ann who met a chap from New Zealand when at university and went back with him to settle there. She was the first of the Pacey family to obtain a degree. We didn't realise that Queenie worked at Bletchley Park. It was only when researching some history about my mother, that we saw her on the register. Neither lady ever spoke to each other about being there.

The name Papworth means papa and enclosure. It originated in Cambridgeshire and can be linked to the Papworth 12th century Lord of the Manor, Papworth Everard. The Papworth Hospital, Cambridge opened as a sanitorium for Tuberculosis in 1918 before developing as a specialist hospital for thoracic surgery during the 1950s. Many Papworths still live in that area. Hepworth and Bosworth are said to be connected names.

My mother's father, Thomas Archibald Papworth, was orphaned at the age of 6 when his parents ironically died of Tuberculosis! They were from a poor butcher's family at Blunden, Bedfordshire. His father died first and his mother 18 months later. I marvel that he did not end up in an orphanage or workhouse. His mother could see what was happening and made provision for him to be brought up by her sister, Mrs Johnson, who lived at Newport Pagnell. His parents' graves are still very visible in Sandy Council Cemetery and have not weathered much. Thomas was a gifted musician, playing both the piano and organ.

Thomas won a scholarship to Bedford Modern School. He took an electrical apprenticeship when he left school and worked at Wolverton Works. He also helped in his aunt's fruit shop. Unfortunately, Thomas was just the right age in 1914 to be called up for the First World War and went into the Royal Engineers. There was a training camp for the Royal Engineers at Staple Hall, Fenny Stratford. We do not know much about his war service as we never saw his medals, and he was very anti uniformed organisations after the war and wouldn't even let my mother join the Girl Guides.

Towards the end of the war Thomas suffered shell-shock and was discharged. Knitting was encouraged to help him be active with his hands and improve his concentration. Unusually for a man, he was taught North Bucks lacemaking, a skill not seen in many men. He continued this hobby for many years. After the war he went back to work as an electrician in the Newport

Grandad Papworth as a choirboy at Newport Pagnell

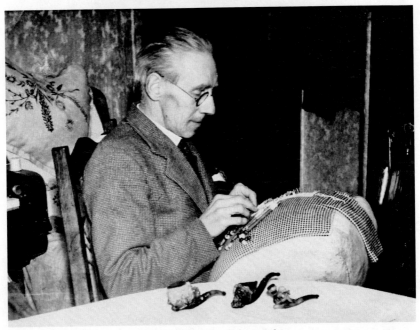

Grandad Papworth lacemaking

17

Pagnell area. He must have met my grandmother on his work around Fenny Stratford. My mother was born in 1922 and christened at St Martin's Church.

Poppy, as he was affectionately called, was organist at St Martin's and its sister Mission Church St Margaret's for over 22 years. When times became tough during the 1930s, they rented a house with a shop at the front, along Aylesbury Street, and ran a fruit business. Both grandparents were very keen on amateur dramatics and feature in local history books of old programmes e.g. 'Yeoman of the Guard' and in photographs of 'The Mikado' taken in the 1930s.

Grandma and Grandad Papworth in 'The Mikado'

Grandma Papworth with tambourine outside Red House where I was born.
Coronation of King George V and Mary in 1911

Great Grandad Blunt outside his butcher's shop in Aylesbury Street, 1905

My maternal grandma, Eveline, grew up with three sisters and a younger brother. They lived by the canal and Nagles Factory, Fenny Stratford. It is thought that her father was a tea blender who travelled around selling the tea... and one day did not come back! Eventually, his widow married a gentleman farmer from Northampton, Mr West. My grandmother helped her grandfather, Mr Blunt, run a butcher and poultry business at 56 Aylesbury Street, Fenny Stratford and she also had to keep house for her mother. Deliveries were made to nearby villages by pony and trap. They were very busy at Christmas making mince pies and giving out a glass of port to their special customers.

Aunt Madge qualifies at Northampton Hospital

The eldest daughter, Madge, trained as a nurse at Northampton General Hospital and after doing some private nursing and district nursing at Raunds, Northamptonshire, later became the Nurse Superintendent to all the nurses and midwives in Hampshire. The second daughter, Connie, became a teacher and later went to live near Leicester. She had a daughter called Heather that Mum liked to keep in touch with. Bernard, the apple of their eye, worked in a bank, but sadly he contracted meningitis and died aged 21 in 1920.

CHAPTER 2
THE FAMILY'S WORK

My father left school at 14 and took a hairdressing apprenticeship. This was in the days when you could train to do ladies' hair as well as men's, so he learnt to do the fashionable Marcel Waves.

At the age of 21 he decided to branch out and start his own business. A shop became available on the main Bletchley Road and my father was able to purchase it. This was, again, by 'the bank of the family' and his three brothers, who like himself had managed to save £100, which was a lot of money in 1936. These brothers would need to be paid back later on. The house was a detached property, well placed in the middle of the main shops and opposite the Conservative Club.

In 1939 events took a turn for the worse and Dad was eventually called up in 1940. He had been given twelve months to find someone to run the business. A retired barber was found, and as his parents were very canny Brits they moved into the rooms at the back of the shop to keep an eye on the trade.

Dad joined the Queen's Royal Regiment of the Royal Artillery, became a bombardier with the big guns and enlisted at Deep Cut Barracks on 12th December 1940. I do not know much about his service, as so many of that era would not talk about the war, but according to his service book he made a will in 1943. He served in the Middle East, North Africa and Italy. How things have changed! The chaps had no ear protection from the loud bangs and no proper protection from the heat of the desert. I have a photograph of Dad taken in the Iraqi dessert in 1942. He would

Dad's Platoon, Iraq, 1942

Dad and Wal in Cairo, 1944

tell the tale of playing his bugle (which he had learned in the Boys Brigade) to frighten away the wolves at night. He did say that it was 40 degrees at midday and 2 degrees at night! They only had a small enamel bowl to wash with and shave and he told us that many became injured and burnt during the fighting there.

Dad became a medical orderly to the medical officer in 1941, so had to stay with the badly injured and administer morphine until they could be taken to a field hospital or died. We have a photo of him with his older brother, Walter, sent to my grandparents from Cairo, when they were able to meet up during 1944. He was only given 48 hours leave in those days – no returning from the battle area to come home on leave! He was able to supplement his income a little by doing the short back and sides of his fellow servicemen. Dad was demobbed in 1946 with a final settlement pay of £25.5s.11d. and a demob suit! As Dad joined up later, so he came out later, as everyone could not return as soon as the war ended.

Dad's testimonial by a Major John Bowles states:

> Military conduct; Exemplary. This man has served for 5 years and has served actively in Africa and Italy. A cheerful man, who gets on well with everybody. Works hard and well and is thoroughly reliable.

Dad did try and keep in contact with some of his local service mates after the war and was a voluntary caretaker at the Bletchley Yeomanry Hall for a number of years.

My mother was an only child and went to Bedford Business College when she left school. There was not much an ordinary girl could do in those days for a career. If you did not want to work in a shop or factory the only other options were to go away and train as a nurse or teacher, as her aunts had done. She caught the train at Fenny Stratford each day and travelled to Bedford. There she became very proficient in shorthand and typing.

Mum's first clerical job was working for Shirley's, a cattle feed merchant. The Fenny Stratford area was very rural at that time and her main task was to send out invoices to the local farmers to remind them to pay their bills.

In 1942 the cry went out for more people to work at Bletchley Park (codenamed Station X). Little did people know that it was a top-secret intelligence centre! The gossip locally was that they were making special parts for radios to help with the war effort. People were told not to ask and to 'keep mum'. They advertised for shorthand typists and as Mum did not want to be called up for the forces she applied, as she thought it was a clerical job. She was 19 years old and would be part of one of the biggest secrets of the war. Everyone was required to sign the 1911 Official Secrets Act and it was impressed on them all how important this was. Even the cleaners, canteen workers and binmen were only told what was essential for their job. They did not realise the significance of the work there. Mother wrote an article for the Bletchley Gazette in 1974 after revelations began to appear nationally about the work.

Bletchley Park Mansion, home of the Codebreakers

The Papworth Trio during the war

My maternal grandfather had a cigarette kiosk outside the canteen for the duration of the war. This was just inside the entrance gate along Wilton Avenue and he did a good trade selling tobacco, matches and cigarettes. In the evenings he could be found running the Papworth Trio, a dance group providing music at a lot of socials. Some were called the 'Penny Hop 'and dances were held in St Martin's Hall, Wilton Hall and The Bletchley Road school hall.

When Mum first went to work at the Park, she was secretary to the Park Fire Officer. This involved sending out reminders for fire practices and fire precautions – as many people smoked and the huts were wooden, it was a constant threat to life and security. They practised with stirrup pumps and how to efficiently do evacuations. Mum later joined many other girls in a cohort to learn Morse Code (and become part of the secret code breaking team). The young women had intensive training for two months so that they could type out Morse without looking at the typewriter keys. Unfortunately, she was biking to the Park one frosty morning in the blackout and fell off her bicycle, fracturing a bone in her ankle, so she was off work for two months and was then put back a set.

My son, who is a teacher, interviewed Mum on film in 2004 when she was in a residential home. She remembered working in each hut for about nine months then being moved to another hut. Mother was very musical, playing both the organ and piano. She told my son how she enjoyed the lunch time concerts at Bletchley Park, one in particular given by Dame Myra Hess. Churchill visited his 'golden goose that never cracked' before she worked there, but she did remember a visit by Admiral

Mum's 21st Birthday while working at Bletchley Park

Sir James Summerville. "Of course, they were given special food; they did not have to eat the food from our canteen!" she said. Two chaps, George and Dennis who were billeted at her parents' home, took a photograph of her on her 21st birthday in the garden. They then enlarged it, so she guessed that they worked in the map reading room and did reconnaissance work at the back of the Park.

Describing the work, Mum explained that the tape came out of the Enigma machines double sided, and once you had lined up the four rotors for the codes that day, typists had to type out the letters coming through. They would note country of origin, mainly Italy or North Africa, and the time sent. They set the prefix of the machine so that it was the same as the person sending it. One side of the tape was coded letters and the other would be the message they typed. It was then glued on full size paper and logged in huge books. The message would be sent via vacuum pipes to other departments. Some messages were stuck on huge boards on the wall. It was thanks to the building of the Bombe and Colossus machines in breaking the daily cypher codes that the messages could be decoded. If the machine broke down you phoned for mechanics to come and worked on another machine. Staff worked in shifts, 8.00 am to 4.00 pm, 4.00 pm to midnight and midnight to 8.00 am, with half an hour for lunch and on nights a breakfast break at 7.00 am.

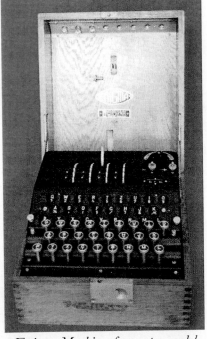

Enigma Machine, four rotor model

Many staff arrived at the Park in five large coaches, which were called 'the western desert', but Mother, after the mishap with her bicycle, would catch the bus at St Martin's Church, Fenny Stratford half an hour before her shift. People were billeted in all the villages around as far as Bedford. I remember that Mum was particularly friendly with a girl called Vera who came from Hanslope, seven miles away, where another secret diplomatic wireless station was based. The Secret listening stations were called Y stations and were scattered all over the globe. Interestingly, Bletchley Park happened to be listening station number ten, hence being known as 'Station X'. There weren't any masts or wire poles at Bletchley Park, but many were placed in the villages nearby. A memorial at Bletchley Park unveiled by HM The Queen in 2011 pays tribute to some of them, including those in nearby villages, Little Horwood, Wavendon and Drayton Parslow.

The only real danger from the unsuspecting enemy would have been if they had bombed the railway station adjoining the Park, as it was an important junction with eight platforms. In those days one could travel almost anywhere from Bletchley. Passengers could get to London Euston in less than an hour, or up to Rugby and Crewe. Across country was the Varsity Line connecting Oxford and Cambridge, so vital for the academics working at the Park during the war years. Later on, my parents would enjoy day trips to Bedford and Northampton along the branch lines. As mentioned previously, Dad's father was a train driver based at Bletchley Station for many years, having worked his way up from the fireman's role. So many people were connected to the station and this is why many of my relatives lived in the terraced houses nearby.

One story my mother would tell was of 16-year-old Tommy Brown who had captured codes from German U-boat 559 in 1942. The captain of *HMS Petard* ordered three sailors to swim to the sinking U-Boat to see if they could rescue any sensitive papers. Tommy managed to retrieve Enigma codes, but sadly the other two sailors drowned in the process. This was on 30th October 1942 and enabled Bletchley Park to break the codes and warn allied shipping where the U-boats would be.

With the *Petard* material and the four-rotor Enigma, U-boat traffic code was broken within six weeks. This eventually helped protect the convoys from America bringing essential food and equipment. Tommy was awarded the George Medal and his sisters didn't know the details why until it became unclassified thirty years later. Sadly, Tommy died three years later when his house in South Shields caught fire. The NAAFI and the community has put a memorial in a community hall there in his honour. The staff register at Bletchley Park enabled us to see the main huts where Mother worked and provides a useful tool for research.

Another of my mother's stories was when she was on duty on Boxing Night 1943 and there was a lot of activity going on in the 'most secret room'. Messages were going backwards and forwards all night long from Bletchley Park to the Admiralty. The British Navy was chasing the German battleship, the *Scharnhorst*, up the North Sea to the Norwegian Fjords. It was sunk there and Mum stayed on to hear this news well past 8.00 am when she could have gone off duty.

My mother's weekly wage was £2.7s.6d. per week. The men doing the same job earned a pound more. The Americans came in and earned £10 per week! Mother felt she could speak about some of her experiences thirty years later when F.W. Winterbotham published his book 'The Ultra Secret'. He was Chief of Air Department Secret Intelligence MI6 from 1930-1945. This let the cat out of the bag! Many accounts followed.

My mother met my father during 1946. They were both local, so probably knew each other vaguely from school, but he was six years older than her. Everyone felt their life had been on hold for six years. She said that his chat up line was, "Would you like to come shopping with me to Northampton?" as he knew girls enjoyed their shopping. His half day closing was on

My parents' wedding at St Martin's, July 1947

Wednesday afternoons so that is when they could do their courting. They married in July 1947, the same year as the Queen, and I was born in 1950. Sometime after the wedding my grandparents moved out and purchased a house next-door to one of their daughters (Auntie Beat, my godmother).

After the war it was difficult to obtain good references, as Mum's work had been top secret, but she managed to get a good job at the Fenny Stratford Police Station where she was secretary to the Police Superintendent. She told the tale of a robbery where they were given an early warning message and were able to phone some Policemen at the other end of Bletchley who apprehended the robbers on their getaway. This was from the blue telephone box, long before any radio-controlled cars! Her biggest disappointment came when, as a married woman, she had to give up that job. Women were expected to stay at home, keep house and look after their husbands! However, later on I was determined to have a career.

CHAPTER 3
A HAPPY CHILDHOOD

I had an unusual childhood really as I grew up in a room behind my father's hairdressing business. I was born on Saturday 17th June 1950, which would have been Dad's busiest work day, but Mother was able to have me at the Red House. This was a small maternity unit at the back of the GP's house and surgery along the Watling Street at Fenny Stratford. It was formerly the stables and had been converted into a three-bedded unit for local cases.

Pacey's Hairdressers 1949

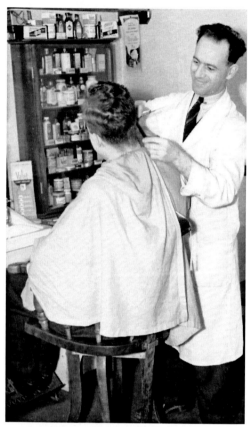

Dad in his shop in the 1950s

My earliest memory is when I was whizzing about on an old tricycle and clumsily ran into a lady doing her shopping at Weatherhead's the grocers opposite our shop. The lady's stockings were torn and Mother gave her some money for a new pair! Dad would sing the war songs when trying to get us to sleep, 'Lili Marlene', 'Wish me luck as you wave me goodbye' and 'Now is the hour for me to say goodbye'. I vaguely remember my granddad (Mother's father) taking me out in the pushchair to watch the steam trains, and he would also take me along the Grand Union Canal at Fenny Stratford to see the barges going through the locks.

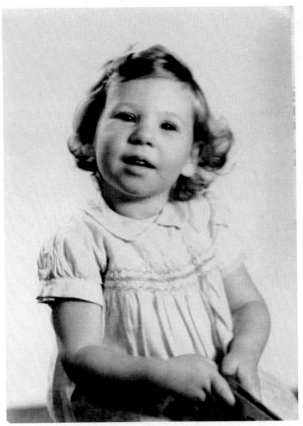

Aged 2… a proper Pacey

When I was about three and a half, Mother took me to Westfield Road to the 'Toc-H' Hut, where a lady ran a small playgroup in the mornings and she tried to teach us some basic numbers, letters and nursery rhymes. It was here that I met one of my lifelong friends, Hazel, and we have kept in touch ever since.

At 4 years old I was eligible to go to the Council Nursery School next to Bletchley Road Infants' School – I can still remember the smell of disinfectant used to clean everything in sight. We had lots of toys, trolleys and bikes to play with and to let off steam. Miss Tofield was one of the young ladies gaining experience with children and she was to become a great influence on most

My first car!

of the pupils' lives later on as our music teacher in the secondary school. After lunch we had a rest on camp beds, before having a story and crayon time.

My sister, Rosemary, was born in December 1954, and I remember in amazement when Mum brought her home how dainty her little fingers and toes were – just like a little doll. I vaguely remember her christening at St Martin's Church with the family all congregated around the font. The party afterwards was held in Dad's shop, where I enjoyed all the attention and people to chat to. Mum told me that my christening was at harvest time to the music of 'Fair Waved the Golden Corn'. It was in the infants' school that I met Dorothy, another lifelong friend, and Dad allowed her to come on holiday with us as he thought it would be good company for me. However, we probably spent most of the time arguing! She remembers that I kept knocking her sandcastles down! I remember one of our infant teachers was married at the Methodist Church opposite

My Christening, September 1950

Dot on the left of me at a clinic aged 11 months old

the school and we were photographed together watching from the gates. We loved to see the beautiful bridesmaids' dresses and guests' outfits.

We did not realise that rationing was still in operation until 1954. A lot of sugar was added to most drinks after it came off ration, especially to tea. 'Camp Coffee' was made from chicory, not the lovely coffee beans that are used today. My friends and I were often dragged to the dentist, as this was before the era of fluoride tablets and we had to have a lot of fillings. I seemed to alternate between the school dentist and Dad's private dentist, Mr Marshall. I shall never forget the awful rubber masks put on my face when my back teeth (molars) were removed, and feeling so groggy, half-awake staggering home holding onto Mum's arm.

The shop was very busy and Dad would nearly always have an apprentice in tow. It was my job after school to come into the shop and sweep up the hair with a dustpan and brush, emptying it all into an old, large, Smiths crisp tin. Dad would sell some chocolate bars or crisps to waiting customers as he had a captive audience. This was when the 6d bags of crisps had a little blue bag inside containing salt, so you added your own amount of seasoning/flavour. As I got older, I was expected to make a tray of coffee and tea to serve to the waiting customers. I didn't mind this as they gave me sixpenny tips, but I had to wash up the cups and saucers afterwards, which was a chore. I would also make up the orders to help Dad send off for more stock from the wholesalers at Dunstable. We sold a lot of cigarettes at that time and I remember one day a box of Swan Vesta matches falling off the shelf and catching alight. Dad quickly stamped out the flames and after that Dad always sold the safety matches.

When toddlers came for their first haircut to trim their beautiful curls, Dad would sit them on their mother's lap and fill the washbasin with little boats and plastic container tops. He would also add some bubbles in the hope of distracting them from their haircut. I liked to watch him sharpening his cut-throat razors on

At Bekonscot with Grandma Papworth,
with Dad and Rosie in the background

a leather strop rubber belt. It was quite a skill to witness him giving a chap a cut-throat shave with his steady hand. At that time, he wore a starched white coat which used to frighten the young children, as they probably thought that he was the doctor or dentist. As soon as nylon tunics became available, he wore those and of course they did not need all the laundering.

There was not much going on for us in the holidays and my sister and I would spend a lot of time walking up and down Bletchley Road looking at the shops. We had a Boots the Chemist nearby, Findlay's sweet shop, Neal's toy shop, Birtel's fruit and pet shop, Pollard's the ironmongers, Home and Colonial for groceries and Iron's for shoes. The only large stores were Woolworths (where we spent a lot of time) and the large

Co-op department store. Father Christmas would arrive there at the beginning of December, which was exciting. Later on, it introduced a coffee bar where we could meet our friends.

Many Italian and Polish men would call in for a haircut on their way to work at the London Brick Company in Newton Longville. They always carried an Oxo tin with their sandwiches in. Other workmen would be on their way to work at the railway station. I remember a man who had just arrived in Britain, who was a Sheikh and wore a turban. Dad had the job of unravelling his long pony tail and cutting the hair off, before he was allowed to start work, due to safety regulations.

During the long summer evenings, I would play tennis, knocking a ball onto the tall wall of the building next-door. In the winter I would try and spend time in the library around the corner. I could sit in the reference library to do my homework, as there was nowhere peaceful at home to do it.

On Saturday mornings we went to the pictures – the Studio Cinema was only about two hundred yards away. All the kids would pile in to watch 'The Little Rascals' film or 'The Lone Ranger'. It was the era of Cowboys and Indians. There were also cartoons to watch and it was only about 6d old money to go in. Sometimes if Mrs Basketfield was the usherette, she would give my sister and me an upgrade in the 9d seats. Dad would go to her house and cut her disabled husband's hair. Dad had a board outside the shop advertising the films to be shown. For this, the cinema gave him two free tickets each week, so the apprentice and my mother would take it in turns to use the tickets. Mum would go with Auntie Gertie and the apprentice with his girlfriend.

Christmas was a happy time. Dad would put large coloured bulbs up in the living room and all along the hallway, and we would make lots of paperchains and streamers to hang around the living room. Every year Rosemary and I would be invited to the Royal Artillery Children's Party held at the Yeomanry Hall in Far Bletchley. We would catch the bus with Mum and she would leave us there with our friends. Dad would collect us after work, so that he could catch up with his Army friends. Father Christmas came and gave us lovely presents and we would enjoy a magic show or an entertainer. The tea would be lots of sandwiches, cakes, jelly and ice cream which was a treat in those days.

On Saturday evenings we would watch 'Dixon of Dock Green' on the little black and white television set. One Saturday evening we heard a noise like breaking glass. Dad told us to sit quietly and he would go to investigate. Sure enough, a youth was breaking into the Castle Wool shop next-door. Dad managed to grab the youth and wedge him into the public telephone box, whilst he dialled 999. The Police came and arrested the chap. He ended up in a Borstal prison as he had done other burglaries and Dad received a commendation letter from the Police Chief Constable.

How Dad ran a business without a telephone I cannot imagine, but like others of his generation, he was a little scared of technology. He did not have a phone until I went nurse training, when he realised it would be the best way to keep in touch.

We were like many other children at the time, going around the rear of the shops and back doors looking for empty glass bottles, as we could take them to the Victoria Wine shop on the corner of Westfield Road and collect 3d per bottle. (Recycling is not a new concept!) Another fond memory of mine is using Dad's old gramophone player whilst he was out at working. He kept his old records under the bath! We would play the Dick Barton theme tune, Gracie Fields songs, 'Bye Bye Blackbird', or 'The Ride of the Valkyries', the records Dad had bought from the 1930s. One day we over wound the gramophone player and broke the spring. We took it across to Weatherheads electrical shop opposite and got a new spring put in. It took five days and used up our pocket money, but hopefully Dad never found out!

Dad purchased a small two-berth caravan and placed it in the back garden and we would play in there with our friends for hours. Sometimes we held tea parties and other times we would pretend to be in a medical unit. Once we were given a puppy and hid it in the caravan, but Mum found it and made us take it back. She did not want a puppy to look after and said that it would get run over on the busy Bletchley Road. However, we were allowed rabbits and a bird. We even tried to look after a tortoise, but it escaped and was never seen again.

When Mum developed an allergy to the budgerigar's feathers, we had to move it to a large cage in the shop. The children loved to talk to 'Joey' and I would clean it out on Sundays with a new sandpaper liner and fresh water, seed and cuttle fish. Sometimes it was given a fly around the shop when the shop was closed. I entered it in the Bletchley Caged Bird Pet Shows and it usually won five shillings, first prize for its class. They said it was because it had lovely black feathers under its chin and pure green feathers on the rest of its body. Sometimes our rabbits would disappear; sadly, Uncle Tom had been around whilst we were at school. He had skinned them so we could have a rabbit pie, as Dad was partial to rabbit pie.

Our routine on Sundays was different to the rest of the week. All the shops were closed and it could be very boring. We went to church and Sunday School first thing – this was at St Margaret's Mission Church on the corner of Brooklands Road where Mum was the organist. When this closed in 1960, we went to the main parish church at Fenny Stratford and Mum went to Soulbury Church to become their organist for 35 years.

After church we would be expected to visit Grandma Pacey in Osbourne Street. She liked to see us growing up and wearing our Sunday best clothes, as she had a lot of grandsons but not many granddaughters. This was quite a walk from Fenny Stratford, so we would visit Auntie Beat on the way, who lived next-door, and she would give us a glass of squash and a freshly baked fairy cake, as Sunday was her baking day. After this we would visit Auntie Nora nearby and she gave us a bar of Fry's Chocolate Cream. Auntie Nora kept a large box just for our visits. She was very grateful to Dad as he displayed her upholstery in his shop window to help her sell it. He was also a handyman and would mend Beat and Nora's washing machines if anything went wrong, or put in new fuses in their plugs etc.

Sunday was Dad's only full day off work, so he would like to get on with some jobs around the house. He would try his hand at anything – repairing the car, painting the walls, mending shelves or sweeping out the chimney. One day when I was walking home from school a girl ran over to me and said, "Your house is on fire!" Sure enough, the fire engine was outside our house. It was a Wednesday afternoon, which was Dad's early closing day, and he had tried to get the soot from the chimney with a set of old brushes. When he relit the fire, some of the brush had got lodged in the chimney and caught alight. The firemen were very good and soon put the fire out and did not make too much mess. It was cups of tea all round for the crew before they left!

Rosemary and I both had piano lessons from the age of 8. Every Thursday after school we would go to a house where our teacher, Miss Spratley, hired the front room. Mum made sure that we practised each evening after tea. This paid off as we were entered into the Royal College of Music Exams, usually one grade each year.

Poor Dad had to put up with our practices and frustrated outbursts on the other side of the shop wall. It cost 3s.6d. (17½p) per half-hour lesson. Our piano playing examinations were held at a house in Bedford, so we would go on the train and walk along the river to the house. Depending on the time of the exam, we would be able to go shopping afterwards. I managed to study as far as Grade 6 and even passed Grade 5 with Distinction. Miss Spratley was so pleased that she sent me a telegram. (The only other telegram that I ever received was a congratulations on my 21st birthday.)

On Bonfire night we would let off fireworks in the garden. Dad would place them on a wooden box and set them off. He nailed Catherine wheels to the trellis fence and we held sparklers with our gloves on. While this was going on, jacket potatoes would be cooking in the oven. We would come inside about 8.00 pm and have tomato soup and then the potatoes. Happy memories!

Mum was always worried that we would become ill. She was old fashioned and dressed us in vests, liberty bodices and flannelette petticoats in the junior school, for which we often got teased. Rosemary and I had the usual childhood infections, but I never caught chickenpox even though we were in the same bedroom. I was taken to Stoke Mandeville Hospital when I was 7 with a kidney infection and was in bed at home with various antibiotics for two weeks suffering rigors and lethargy. The doctor said that the next time this happened Dad was to go and phone for an ambulance.

I will always remember that Sunday afternoon when the cream-coloured ambulance sped me along to Ward 14 at Stoke Mandeville. The first few days there I was not interested in anything; not even sweets which were counted out of a tin after lunch. All sweets and chocolate had to be handed in so that they could be shared around. New antibiotics were coming on the market and the doctors must have been able to give me a better one than the GP had tried previously. Two overseas nurses gave me a bed bath and I marvelled at their large hands and pink palms, not having seen any Caribbean people before. I was coaxed to eat jelly and ice cream, and little sandwiches cut in the shapes of trees and balls. This was the first time that I had been offered two eggs for breakfast, long before the days of the array of cereals we can have today. Each day I would sit on a draw sheet, which was placed over the bedclothes, feeling depressed. I could watch, through the window, some of the children playing with the toys and swinging outside, as it was the August holidays. When I was allowed up, two nurses held me one each side in case I felt dizzy or fell.

Visiting was very strict. Mum and Dad would visit on Wednesday afternoons when the shop was closed, and Mum and Auntie Gert would visit on Saturdays coming on the bus to Aylesbury then catching another bus to the hospital. Grandma would visit on Sunday afternoons, with my sister waving to me from outside as she was not allowed into the ward.

I went home after three weeks and the doctors said to give me the first week off school. Mum had rebooked our week away to Margate so we went later. The problem when I went back to school was that I had moved to the Juniors and the new teachers did not know who I was when I went into the classroom with my friends. Mum should have gone with me to explain or sent me with a letter.

Start of Junior School, 1957

If we became ill, we would visit Dr Gleave at his surgery opposite the school. We had to sit in his packed, smoke-filled surgery and wait our turn to see him, as there were no appointments in those days. Anyone seriously ill was taken to Stoke Mandeville or Northampton Hospitals. Later on, an outpatient clinic was built in Whalley Drive, as Bletchley did not have a hospital and this helped. When Grandma Papworth became ill, with a weak heart, she took to her bed. (On reflection, it would have been better if she had been encouraged to exercise to make the heart muscle stronger.) Mum made an extra dinner in the holidays and I would take it to her on my Triang scooter. This was a big, heavy affair. Two plates were tied together to keep the food hot and balanced in a string bag, and I would be expected to whiz up two streets and deliver it. Grandma was only 63 at the time but acted older.

Our holidays consisted of a long weekend at Easter or Whitsun, depending on how late Easter fell. This would be to Dad's two caravans at Hopton-on-Sea, near Great Yarmouth. We would scrub the caravan clean, air the blankets and check the equipment, and any breakages of crockery and cutlery would be replaced. If the weather was good, we would spend time along the coast and explore the beaches. It was usually too cold to swim. If the weather was bad, we might go to Lowestoft and visit the surplus goods at the Army and Navy stores then have fish and chips. Dad would buy us several annuals to read and take home, as they were often selling at half price from Easter. At Great Yarmouth we loved to visit the fun fair and go on the big dipper. Sometimes we would go to the cinema, circus, or the model village.

Our main holiday would be a week during August. It would be Mum's job to book and plan this. She wanted to see different parts of the country, so I can remember weeks at Margate, Bournemouth, Llandudno, Newquay, Blackpool, Paignton and Hastings. It was on our Newquay visit that the car broke down.

The journey was too much for the poor thing, as Dad never had it serviced, only doing what he could do himself. The car went into a garage for the week, so we went on buses or walked that holiday. Mum would try and book bed and breakfast from Sunday to Sunday, as Dad would only want to close the shop on one Saturday (the busiest day for a barber).

As my birthday was in June, I could have a party in the garden. Dad would put up one of his old, green, ridge tents for us to play in and Auntie Gert would come along and help Mum prepare the sandwiches and also help Mum control all the kids! I tried to have a theme for the party each year. One year it was a fancy-dress and the girl that dressed up as the Queen of Hearts had a lovely costume and won. I was only Miss Daily Mirror and my sister had her dressing up nurse's outfit on. The next year it was a maypole theme and we put many ribbons around Dad's tent pole. We had some country dancing tunes on the old wind up gramophone and danced around in our pretty summer dresses.

Fancy Dress for my 10th Birthday Party

The third year we dressed up for a mock wedding, and I also had a pretend fortune teller, using the goldfish bowl as her screen.

Our teachers at the junior school were a mixed bunch. Miss Fowler was a very old-fashioned strict teacher and gave us a slap with the ruler for the slightest misdemeanour. Mr Burns was lovely and helped us understand mathematics and we learnt our times tables well with him. Miss Capel, another old teacher, took us on outings to Whipsnade Zoo and to a country dancing festival at the Royal Albert Hall. Mr Shaw left us halfway through the final year (perhaps he had enough of teaching or obtained a better position), so we had a variety of teachers to cover the rest of the term until the summer holidays.

After the 11-plus we would go our separate ways, some to the Grammar School and some to the Secondary Modern School. I remember the excitement that year when Yuri Gagarin was the first man to orbit in space! Even then, I would carry a little case to school containing First Aid items, so if anyone needed a plaster I could give it to them – a nurse in the making! Our teachers would send anyone with a nose bleed to see me as the first port of call. There was no Matron or any appointed teachers for health and safety in those days, and no accident books or forms etc.

CHAPTER 4
TEENAGE YEARS

I really enjoyed the variety of subjects at the Leon County Secondary School, when we moved classrooms for each lesson and our timetable was varied. Music, drama and art were encouraged and I thrived in the routine, with many facilities and different teachers. Our school choir led by Miss Tofield was excellent, and we sang at the Eisteddfod in Northampton one year. I attended the drama club and was chosen for two of the school plays produced by Olive Gibbs, our brilliant drama teacher. One was Arnold Ridley's, 'The Ghost Train'. Mr Morris, our art teacher let us use pictures for mosaics and

The Ghost Train School Production

gave us a taster at trying clay work. Mr Cross inspired us to study Geography, encouraging us to go to evening classes for RSA exams (Royal Society of Arts) in Geography and English. Mr Buck Jones taught us English, and Mr Puryer (another strict teacher) taught us Maths, which I found dull and challenging.

The daily assemblies were inspiring, and Mr Morris was tasked with playing popular classical music when we marched into the hall each morning. This could be works by Handel, Elgar, Mendelssohn or Grieg. Sometimes I played the hymns on the piano for the assembly if Miss Tofield was doing something else. Mr Bradshaw was a Methodist and gave us many tips for life. One of his sayings that I have tried to take on board was, "Don't waste time. One can get money back by earning more, but time can never be brought back. It's your most precious commodity." Another thought was to, "Appreciate good teachers." Some would be kind and others inspiring and show leadership. These were the people that one remembers in later life and I feel lucky to have met many inspiring mentors throughout my years, as we are all lifelong learners.

I enjoyed going abroad with the school for the first time to Switzerland, where we loved the mountains and lakes, the cows with the bells around their necks and the geraniums flowering on the window boxes. I bought a little musical box to keep as a souvenir, and enjoyed my first proper 'steak, mushrooms and chips' at a restaurant on the way home through Berne where we saw live bears in a pit, the symbol of the city.

My sister, Rosemary came on the next holiday to Holland. Mr Bradshaw, the headmaster, led this trip. I remember a terrific thunderstorm one night in which we all held hands, scared in our dormitory bedroom, until it passed. We were taken to a Delft pottery factory, and of course we brought back some little clogs as a souvenir. To enable us to have school trips, Dad hired out camping equipment, roof racks and caravans, as domestic travel grew in popularity.

As I grew older Dad bought extra 'mod cons' for the family. Later, we had an egg machine, sweet machine and milk machine in the little front porch. We felt fortunate as we always had a car when not many families had transport. These cars were always second or third hand. One in particular he was very proud of. It was a Humber Hawk and had only one previous owner, the local doctor!

On Sunday afternoons Mum would take us on walks around Bletchley. In the summer we would often visit Auntie Gertie and go to watch the cricket with her husband at the Rodex Coat Factory grounds off Denbigh Road. During the winter we would stay indoors and watch the Bing Crosby, Dorothy Lamour films, 'On the Road to Singapore' etc, never dreaming that one day we would visit those exotic places. Sunday evenings we would have our baths to the music of 'Sing Something Simple', get our uniforms ready for the week and tidy the bedroom.

My Birthday Party c1963

Mum belonged to several groups, including the Mothers' Union, Women's Institute, and the George Street Community Centre Ladies Choir. Over the years Mum encouraged me to sing at the shows and concerts performed by these groups. My party pieces included, 'Bless this House', 'Mary's Boy Child' and 'Jerusalem'.

We walked backwards and forwards to school four times each day, as most of us went home for lunch. Poor Dorothy had the longest walk of all my friends, all along Bletchley Road as far as the Park Hotel near the station and down Duncombe Street. Another good friend of mine was Hazel, whom I first met at the nursery and she lived near my grandma, so I played at Hazel's house frequently on a street called, The Crescent. When my mother was visiting my grandma, we would play with the other children on the grassed areas. Later we went on days out and we have kept in close touch over the years.

Looking back now, our diet was fairly poor during my teenage years and a lot richer too – it consisted of full cream milk, lard (saved from the Sunday joint) and butter. Quite a lot of the meals were fried and most adults smoked. Dad later developed cancer of the bladder, which the consultant told him had probably been a consequence of passive smoking, inhaled from the customers whilst working in the shop.

This was our life until 1965, when Dad had worked 35 years since leaving school at 14 and wanted to sell-up and retire. He often had letters from developers wanting to purchase the property as it was in a very favourable spot for retail business. The house and shop were finally sold to Jim Marshall, the owner of a factory at Fenny Stratford that made electric guitars and amplifying equipment. He wanted a front to display his goods and turned it into a much bigger shop where he later won retail awards in his industry. His two sons carried on the business until the shop was later sold and turned back into two smaller shops.

When the offer came, Dad bought a bungalow in quieter Woburn Sands with some of the proceeds. There was going to

Bletchley Road in the early 1960s

be a lot of building and development in the area as a new city, Milton Keynes, was planned for North Bucks. Woburn Sands was chosen for two reasons: firstly, he heard of a shop going where he could conduct some business part-time and, secondly, Woburn Sands was on a branch line which would help us all get into Fenny Stratford or Bedford for shopping.

Dad spent a few months trying to modernise the 1930s bungalow on Weathercock Lane. He extended the kitchen from the outside toilet and shed, and put in a new turquoise coloured bathroom suite, which was highly fashionable at the time. He treated Mum to a new Hammond Organ, which was installed into the front room, but it was only a two-bedroomed property so Rosemary and I still shared a bedroom!

However, I was about to start my O Level year, so wanted to stay at Leon School. A school bus drove around the villages, and Woburn Sands was usually the first pick up, as Armstrong's coaches were based there. We needed to be at the crossroads by the Swan Hotel by 8.00 am. Mr Armstrong did not stand any

Our shop after we moved to Woburn Sands

bad behaviour or rowdiness, and he would stop the bus and threaten to tell Mr Bradshaw, who also lived in Woburn Sands. I would try and refresh homework and keep my head down on the journeys, as it passed through Wavendon and Bow Brickhill. If we went to an after-school club, we would go to Fenny Station and catch the train back home.

When I reached my 16th birthday, many of my friends were already 16 so we went to the pub at the bottom of Weathercock Lane and bought some cider to celebrate, as 16 was the magical age that cider could be purchased!

There was only nine of us in the sixth form and transferring to the grammar school wasn't an option in those days, so we didn't

The Pacey Clan at Woburn Sands

get many taught lessons and did a lot of private study. Looking back, it was like a gap year from school to work. A week of extra tuition at County Farm, Aylesbury, proved successful as I passed my O Level Cookery and Nutrition soon afterwards. I spent some time in the commerce class and passed the O Level Commerce, and sometime in the technical class to study Biology. Some of the pupils who had left school at 15 started family life early. One day as we were looking out of the windows in our form room at the back of the stage, we saw one of our friends pushing a pram! Another girl married her childhood sweetheart, with the parents' blessing, and emigrated to Canada shortly afterwards to do missionary work with the Baptist Church.

With my friends at Leon School

My heart became set on nursing and I had the aim of going to the world-renowned Stoke Mandeville Hospital. That last summer holiday was spent working in the plastics factory at Woburn Sands and going to parties to say goodbye to friends. My new life was about to take off!

CHAPTER 5
A LIFELONG AMBITION

Most people have heard of Florence Nightingale and Mary Seacole, but it was Ethel Gordon Fenwick who formalised nurses' training and improved their working conditions. In 1881 she became Matron of St Bartholomew's Hospital and campaigned for the next thirty years for a nationally recognised register for nurses. This was achieved in 1919.

"Don't stand there like wet penguins doing nothing... get on with some work," the sister shouted from her office to Otway and me. We had come to the Men's Medical Ward from the Preliminary Training School for two hours to gain some experience. We stood in the middle of the men's ward, with a lot of male patients who were grey in colour. We were surrounded by tubes and men connected to oxygen cylinders and we did not have a clue what to do. Fortunately, a staff nurse and a third-year student nurse came to rescue us and we spent the afternoon working with them. Margaret Otway's father was an ambulance man and often brought patients into the ward. Her mother belonged to the St John Ambulance and was the first casualty that I encountered, when entering the First Aid Competitions as a Bletchley cadet.

I so desperately wanted to become a nurse. My mother suggested that I train at Northampton where Aunt Madge had trained, but I was having none of it. Always the rebel, I wanted to go somewhere else. Stoke Mandeville Hospital was world-famous, specialising in spinal injuries, and also it had a famous plastic surgery speciality that provided a vital service during the war.

Having learned the basics of bedmaking, bandaging and taking observations at St John Cadets, I wanted to be off! Alas, one could not start student nurse training until 18 years of age. I wrote to the Matron at Stoke Mandeville when I was 14 years old and she invited me along in the school holidays to be given a tour of the wards by a sister tutor. The only problem with that was she wanted me to keep in touch and send her an update twice a year on how I was progressing at school. I wonder if she ever read my letters? Her personal secretary must have had a good laugh at my tales. When I was 16 a letter came inviting me for an interview. I did not know what to expect. My school, Leon Secondary, was just starting a sixth form, but it was my father who wanted me to leave school and get a job. He was worried that I would not work and would just waste time.

The interview was quite daunting. There was a panel of three interviewers, the Sister Tutor, Matron and Assistant Matron, all asking me questions. The following questions were fired at me whilst my mother had to sit in the corner of the room:

"What books do you read?"
"What hobbies do you have?"
"Why do you want to be a nurse?"
"What's your favourite subject at school?"
"What is your father's occupation?"
"Where do you go on your holidays?"
"What newspapers do you read?"

Ultimately, they wanted to know if I was temperamentally suited to a nursing career.

After another tour of the wards and a look at the School of Nursing classrooms, I was called back to Matron's office. They seemed happy to reserve me a place when I became 18, but

Stoke Mandeville Hospital

Pre-nursing, January 1968

suggested I spend another year at school and then move to the hospital to become a pre-nursing student.

When I set off with my parents on that Sunday afternoon in September 1967 to check into the Nurses' Home, I was filled with excitement. My father had given me a transistor radio, I had a new house coat, a vanity case filled with toiletries and an alarm clock from my mother. (After leaving school, I had worked in the Plysu Factory at the bottom of the road in Woburn Sands to earn some money to begin my new adventure.)

Stoke Mandeville was founded originally as a small isolation hospital, mainly to cope with outbreaks of Scarlet Fever in the locality. It expanded at the beginning of the Second World War to become one of the official hospitals for the expected casualties, opening on 18th November 1940.

The barrack-style huts were built shortly before the war and the operation was taken over by a branch of the Ministry of Pensions. The Spinal South Corridor was mainly constructed from cedar wood paid for by the Canadian government. Buildings constructed for ten years actually lasted over fifty years until the New Wing was built in the 1980s. Finally, a new hospital has been constructed for the 21st century.

Pre-nursing was very pleasant but we did not earn much money. The first month when I went with the other pre-nurses to the Pay Office, I was given £9 for the month. Pay was in cash in those days.

I loved pre-nursing and found it easy. We only worked from 9.00 am until 4.00 pm and went home at weekends. I lived in the North Nurses' Home with my own little bedroom, which was a pleasure, having always had to share a bedroom with my sister Rosemary, who was four and half years younger than me.

The Nurses' Home consisted of long huts with two bathrooms, and a row of washbasins at the end of the corridor as there were no showers in the 1960s. Also, there was a basic kitchen where we could make a hot drink, heat up soup or have a sandwich. In those days our meals were included in the board and lodging and we were expected to go to the dining room for the three main meals. The kitchen included a twin-tub washing machine, and another corridor had an ironing room and large airing cupboard. All our uniforms were laundered at the hospital laundry.

We spent three months rotating around areas and it was a wonderful way of getting to know how a hospital worked. My first placement was at the Hydrotherapy Pool on the Spinal Injury Unit of the hospital. I had to help the patients get dressed and undressed for the swimming and exercise sessions and some were children on trolleys. Sometimes, out of hours, private patients would pay to use the pool and this helped the finances of the hospital. One man was disabled and came from a wealthy family at Chesham. Some were youngsters crippled with polio and the water would help stimulate their muscles.

Next, I was sent to the Central Sterile Supply Department (CSSD). This was where they sterilised all the instruments and dressings in the autoclave. I did not like the smell there and the monotonous work of packing gauze swabs and cotton wool balls. This was run by a strict sister, but her deputy, a charge nurse, would often let me off early on a Friday to catch the No 144 green bus home to Woburn Sands.

Back at the hospital, Miss Evans was in charge of the sewing room. Our coffee coloured dresses had to be so many inches from the ground and below our knees. Woe betide anyone who tore or damaged the uniforms or if we put on weight or lost it! We were given a nurse's cape, but had to provide our own navy cardigans and brown lace-up shoes.

I was given a fob watch and nurses' dictionary by well-wishers when I left home. Our reading list for homework included Florence Nightingale biographies, Thor Heyerdahl about the Kon-Tiki Expedition and some Dickens novels. No one ever checked if we had read them! Canon Byard, the Vicar of St Mary's Church, Aylesbury had the job of speaking to us once a month in the Nurses' Home. He spoke on morals, but today it is more about nursing ethics. We used to giggle sometimes as he had a funny voice, but I enjoyed those sessions.

One day and one evening a week we would travel to Aylesbury College for study. A regular hospital transport service was provided by the hospital for employees, as Stoke Mandeville was out of town and not many of the poorly paid hospital workers could afford a car in those days. We studied English, Cookery, Maths, Human Biology and Sociology. Although I had the five O Levels required for State Registration, I was entered for the Biology and Sociology exams at Aylesbury College and passed. I also won the Pre-nursing Prize at college, which consisted of choosing two books that I would require for nursing.

Stoke Mandeville had quite a few refugees and displaced persons working at the hospital doing all the jobs that no one else wanted to do i.e. hospital porters, mortuary assistants, gardeners and orderlies. It was the 1960s and there were plenty of jobs, so no one was keen to do the lowly paid unsocial jobs. I became friendly with a chap from Lithuania who was a porter from the CSSD and we skipped off one day on a coach trip to Longleat – I just hoped that neither of us would be missed!

Some Friday evenings I would stay at the hospital to attend the monthly dance in the Nurses' Gymnasium opposite the Nurses' Home. It was a way of getting to know not only the staff, but the local lads. Some of the nurses on night duty would come from the wards in their uniform for the last hour, 11.00 until midnight. All the pop tunes of the '60s were played by the bands and it would end with 'The Last Waltz' by Engelbert Humperdinck.

My third pre-nursing placement was at the Spinal Occupational Therapy. Many patients came for rehabilitation, in particular to learn how to use the Possum Machines. The company was founded in 1961 when a young engineer called Reginald Maling became a volunteer at the National Spinal Injuries Centre. He encountered a young man who had been injured in a water-skiing accident and was totally paralysed from the neck down, and with very little voice – he could only signal to nurses by blowing on a whistle hung near his mouth. Maling designed a device which could be operated by sucking and blowing on a mouthpiece, enabling the patient to activate mechanisms for turning the light on or operating the TV. Later versions could even operate an electric typewriter. He called his invention Patient Operated Selector Mechanism or POSM. Based on this, the word Possum is Latin for 'I can' and was chosen as the name for the company. Frequently the twelve pre-nursing students would be sent to the spinal wards at 12.00 noon to sit and feed the patients their lunch.

Sir Ludwig Guttmann arrived at Stoke Mandeville Hospital in 1944, having fled from Germany with his family because he was a German Jew. His mission was to take charge of a new spinal injury unit and treat servicemen injured during the Second World War. Prior to this the outlook for anyone with a spinal injury was bleak, as they developed horrific bed sores, pneumonia, contractures of the muscles and bladder infections. These mostly were caused by the patient being kept still in bed. He revolutionised the care and would not take no for an answer. Teams of orderlies were employed to turn the patients every two hours and use many pillows to make special pillow pack beds. Regular physiotherapy and breathing exercises were introduced in order to keep the muscles and ligaments healthy. He also reduced the sedation, got them sitting up when able and, weather permitting, placed them outside.

The next hurdle to overcome was how to treat the psychological care of his flock. By now nicknamed 'Papa Guttman', he found that sport restored the kick of adrenaline and reminded the young men that they could still meet their challenges. The first

If I ever did one good thing in my career, it was to introduce sport into the rehabilitation of disabled people 🙶🙷

Professor Sir Ludwig Guttmann, Pioneer

Paralympic Games were held in 1948 to coincide with the Olympic Games and had just 16 competitors. One year later other competitors arrived from other parts of the UK, and in 1952 the Netherlands sent a team and the International Stoke Mandeville Games were born. Stoke Mandeville Sports Stadium was opened by HM The Queen in 1969. It now has a small Heritage Centre explaining the start of the Games. Sir Ludwig is quoted as saying, "If I ever did one good thing in my medical career, it was to introduce sport into the rehabilitation of disabled people." When he died in 1980, 43 countries were participating in the Paralympic Games.

I remember the Games well as they were held on the sports field at the back of the hospital. Competitors and their support staff stayed in run-down huts at the back of the hospital long before the plush Olympic Village was built. This was situated past the mortuary and the animal compound, as mice and other animals were kept for research in those days. We were tasked to push a refreshment trolley around and keep offering Robertson's lemon or orange barley to the competitors – this helped combat dehydration. On glorious July days our mission was to encourage fluids, but of course plenty of chatting up with visitors and athletes alike took place.

One day a bright young man asked me if I would like to go with him to the Royal Festival Hall for an evening concert, as he had two tickets, and I jumped at the chance. He worked next to the OT department in the Bio Medical Laboratory. Of course, we got back late on the returning London train, but I didn't seem to have any problem getting into the Nurses' Home or going to work the next morning.

Coming in or going out!

Because the Nurses' Home was a flat hutted building, climbing into it was easy. If a nurse wanted to return late from the cinema or a date and didn't get a late pass, she would leave the window in her room ajar. The study table would be positioned by the window and the chair next to it. Coming back late at night, we would just lift the chair out, climb onto it and then climb onto the table. After we brought the chair in and shut the window, we could turn the light on. We couldn't shout to the other girls in their bedrooms or the Home Warden might hear us. Her name was Miss Sergeant and we tried to keep out of her way.

CHAPTER 6
A STUDENT NURSE

Being a student nurse was a different ball game and I found the shifts, the expectations of the sisters and the education school hard. The hours had just been dropped from a 44-hour week to 42 hours, but they still had the split shifts. The shifts were 7.30 am – 4.30 pm and split shifts, 7.30 am – 12.30 pm, 4.30 – 8.30 pm. usually on a split shift I would do some ironing, or reading, then have a sleep before going back for the latter half of the shift.

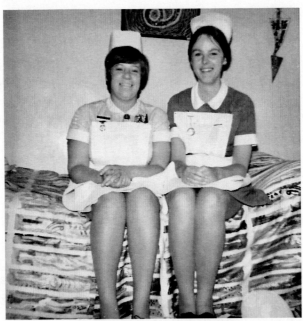

Nurses' home and saggy bed!

The first two months of the training were called 'Going into PTS', which was the Preliminary Training School at the School of Nursing. We had many lectures and sessions on dummies in the practical room. We also learnt how to make beds to a high standard, with the fold at the top being 18 inches and the pillowcases opening away from the door. The basic bed should have two pillows, two cellular blankets and a bedspread, and with all the beds made with crisp envelope corners, the ward would look neat and tidy. This was fine in theory but not very helpful when we were short of linen on the wards.

Mr Robbins, the Hospital Manager, came to visit one of the early blocks in the School of Nursing – he was a friend of my Uncle Wal and apparently played tennis with him. Mr Walker, our tutor, pointed me out to him. "Yes, this is Miss Pacey." "Oh," he said, "...I'm very pleased to meet you, as I play in tennis tournaments with your uncle." Apparently, this entitled them to tickets for Wimbledon. Later on, a nurse spoke to me on the ward saying there was a Mrs Pacey on her ward, was it any relation? I went to see who it was. It was Auntie Queenie, Wal's wife, in for an operation, so I had a nice chat to her.

A suggestion from Mr Walker was to let the patients' feet soak in a bowl for a few minutes when they were stuck in bed for long periods. With often only three nurses to wash all the patients this was not very practical. Many more bed baths were given years ago because patients stayed in bed longer. With better facilities now the patient is able to use the bathroom with support and is more ambulant. Many a new nurse has made the mistake of collecting up all the false teeth for cleaning and then not knowing whose they were. Often a nurse would collect the mercury thermometers and place them in hot water where they would break. Digital thermometers with a disposable cover to be placed in the patient's ear, has made taking observations much easier, in conjunction with the observation stand for recording blood pressure and oxygen levels.

We were kept busy with essays to write and small exams at the end of each week. We would go into the school for various training blocks throughout the three years, being required to pass the drug exam after the first year and the main hospital finals and SRN exams at the end of the three years. In addition, clinical nurse tutors would visit us on the wards and watch us perform various procedures. We would have assessments on patient care for a particular patient and ward management skills.

Nurses needed to gain proficiency in the aseptic technique of cleaning wounds and applying dressings. Forceps or tweezers were used, so as not to touch anything with the hands. Now gloves are used and dressing techniques have changed. Masks were worn and the dressing trolley was required to be spotlessly clean.

Dressing packs would be tipped onto the top shelf – other packs and lotions were positioned on the bottom shelf. Notes and charts were kept at the end of the bed, but are now kept in the notes trolley or on-line. Drugs were always checked by two nurses and dispensed from the drug trolley, but now the patient's own medication is often kept in a locked cupboard at the side of the bed.

It was on that Men's Medical Ward that I saw my first dead body. A young man in his thirties had a heart attack and the doctors tried to do a manual stimulation of the heart by opening him up, but he could not be saved. Everyone was upset and I was designated to learn how to prepare his body and lay him out. It was a third-year student nurse from Mauritius that I worked with and she showed me what to do. Some nurses were quite superstitious and many would not put vases of red and white flowers on the lockers. Some believed that everything including deaths came in threes. The body would be left for an hour to allow the soul to leave the body before it was taken to the mortuary. Curtains would be closed around the other beds and two porters would arrive pushing a silver boxed trolley with a blanket over the top. After they had departed and the nurses remade the bed, the ward would be quiet and subdued for a time.

The next day I was travelling home on the green No 141 bus from Aylesbury to Bedford that conveniently ran along Weathercock Lane at Woburn Sands outside my parents' bungalow. On the bus I heard some women speaking about the patient and how tragic it was. This brought home to me the importance of confidentiality, as you never know who might be listening on a bus.

The next placement was on Ward 9, the Men's Surgical Ward, which became my favourite ward. The ward roster list was put on the noticeboard at the beginning of each month so that we could prepare for the next practical nursing experience.

We were all issued with a General Nursing Council Practical Experience Record Book that had to be filled in by the sister or staff nurse during the placement. A tick by a procedure would indicate the student had seen or watched a treatment. When this was crossed over it indicated that the nurse had become proficient in that task.

On the medical wards this could be giving inhalations, care of a person in an oxygen tent, diabetic diets or chest aspiration. On the surgical wards we would become proficient with special dressings, the removal of sutures and clips, and the post-op care of someone recovering from a prostatectomy.

I enjoyed giving pre- and post-op care. This was before the days of a purpose-built day surgery unit. It seems incredible now but day patients would go to theatre and come back to the ward and recover on another patient's bed with just a draw sheet covering the bedding. The other patient would be sitting down the end of the ward perhaps recovering from a hernia repair or a haemorrhoidectomy.

It was also before recovery rooms were built in theatres. We brought the patient from the operating theatre unconscious and lying on their side with the airway still in situ. They would have their own nurse until they became conscious. Very ill patients were placed in beds by the Sister's Office and as they got better they were moved down the ward and replaced by other patients. Some infected or very ill patients were placed in one of the two side rooms.

The ward had 22 beds, in the open Florence Nightingale style with two side wards. Armchairs and extra cupboards were placed down the middle of the wards. Men would often sneak to the toilet to have a crafty cigarette and the two bathrooms at the end of the ward would be used for men to soak in warm water with a Savlon sachet added. They would be given a shave of the prepared op-site by Mohammad, the orderly.

I worked two of the four Christmases whilst training at the hospital. Numbers on the two men's surgical wards would be cut to a minimum and would combine to close one ward. A side room was decorated and refreshments placed on a long table. I do not know where the bed went for two or three days! Shifts were shared by those covering the ward that Christmas, and wards were allowed to be decorated. On Ward 9 we had a signpost that read, 'Hernia Hill', 'Prostate Walk' and 'Gastro Road'. Sometimes the consultant would come to the ward to carve the turkey at 12.00 noon, which would be before his family's Christmas dinner. Staff would visit the colleagues on other wards and sample their goodies. Some alcohol was allowed at that time. At the weekends we could serve Guinness to the men, which helped to raise their iron levels. Whisky would help dilate the blood vessels and sherry would help improve the appetite.

We had a lovely 'well to do' gentleman who was very ill and was not expected to survive, but remarkably he recovered and on discharge gave each of the ward staff a lovely, boxed, fresh orchid – I had never encountered a real orchid before. Another chap kept coming back to the ward for daily dressings as his

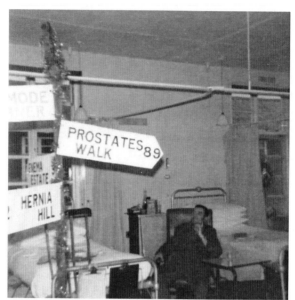

Our Christmas theme Ward 9

Carol singing around the wards on Christmas Eve

wound would not heal. He gave a large box of tights for all the female nurses to share and handkerchiefs for the male staff. As it was mostly chocolates and thank you cards that the ward received, this was a lovely gesture.

It was rewarding to witness the quick recovery and improvement after operations, especially when emergency admissions came in and were taken straight to theatre. This might be for a perforated gastric ulcer or appendicitis. The two men's surgical wards would take it in turns to be 'on take' every other week for emergencies.

Much of the work on the Men's Surgical Ward tended to be for Urology conditions. Many men came to the ward with enlarged prostates or cancer of the prostate, to undergo prostatectomies. Some came with cancer of the bladder. In those days we also had many men coming in with bowel cancer and a large operation called 'abdominal perineal excision of the rectum' was performed. This was an operation taking out a lot of the bowel and giving the patient a colostomy. This is an artificial opening to the skin where a bag is worn to collect the faeces. This procedure was supposed to prolong life in patients, but I do not know that it was very successful. They required a lot of careful nursing and a lot of psychological support. This was the ward that I returned to later as Staff Nurse and then Junior Sister.

Nursing has changed a great deal since the 1960s and '70s. In those days it was task led, such as giving the washes, the observations and the drugs. This gave routine and a feeling of security to the nurses and patients.

Since the Project 2000 degree course, nurses are required to think for themselves and much of the work is evidence based. In 2012 the Chief Nursing Officer set out a vision for nursing, calling for the 'Six Cs' – Care, Compassion, Competence, Communication, Courage and Commitment. The first 18 months are theoretical and the students are supernumerary on the wards. Many student nurses become bank or agency health care assistants to help fund their course and to gain the practical experience on the wards during the three years.

CHAPTER 7
A STUDENT NURSE – PART 2

Other three-month placements included the Female Medical and Surgical Wards, the Paediatric Unit and the Gynaecology Ward. The Orthopaedic Wards and outpatient experience were at the Royal Bucks Hospital, and the Ear Nose and Throat Ward and Chest Wards were at Tindal Hospital. This had been the old workhouse and patients did not like going there. It had been used to house a lot of patients suffering from Tuberculosis and had some chalet type rooms and bi-folding doors for the patients to be wheeled out into the fresh air!

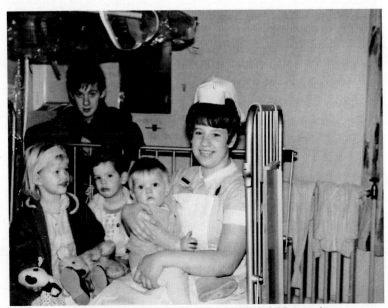

Ear Nose and Throat Ward, Tindal Hospital

I loved working on the Ear Nose and Throat Unit as it had small male and female wards and another section for children having tonsils removed and adenoidectomies. Other children had grommets inserted into their ears for recurrent ear infections. We were allowed to gain experience in the theatre there and, after observing, were allowed to help pass the instruments for the tonsil and adenoid operations. Afterwards we had to observe the children for bleeding and coax them to have Aspirin gargles for their sore throats and try some ice cream and jelly.

One day a little boy was admitted whom, they said, had had his throat mauled by a bear! This was before Milton Keynes Hospital was built. Woburn Safari Park had recently opened and the boy had wound his window down at the back of the car and the bear had managed to claw his throat. He was not badly injured and was only in for observation and to get over the shock. Some children would get the croup badly and were admitted to be nursed in a steam tent.

Another time Matron came to the ward to ask for a volunteer to help on the Chest Ward as they were short staffed. I volunteered as my friend Dorothy was working there and I thought that it would be good to catch up with her, but unfortunately when I went to the ward it was to help with the last offices (laying someone out who had died).

Some adults would come for sinus washouts and throat conditions. One chap was dying with cancer of the throat and we did so enjoy us chatting to him about our off-duty escapades with our friends. I like to think that it cheered him up and made his last days more tolerable. The Florence Nightingale Hospice at Stoke Mandeville Hospital had yet to be built, but Dame Cicely Saunders' ideas of specialist, end of life care were starting to be embraced and I remember a lecture about Helen House, the Children's Hospice in Oxford being taught to us. I had secretly hoped to win the ENT prize at the nurses' annual prize-giving, but was pipped at the post by Janet Maloney and came second!

The long hours and the tiredness took its toll, and I had put on weight due to comfort eating from some of the stressful situations. After a bout of tonsillitis, when I was admitted to sick bay, 'Uncle Bill' the staff doctor let me stay for three weeks on a 600-calorie diet to lose some weight, which helped me lose twelve pounds.

Periods of night duty also helped my weight, as I was not very hungry at night. We worked eight nights on and six nights off. I remember doing three months on a Geriatric Ward one year (now called medicine for older people), three months on the Men's Surgical and the final three months of night duty on the Men's Medical Ward.

The consultant on the Medical Ward was very old school. Everything had to be in order when he did his round or there would be trouble. There was to be absolute quiet, and if a clock could be heard it would need to be removed. Medical students and junior doctors often came to Stoke Mandeville Hospital from the Royal Free Hospital, London. They were instructed to watch, listen and learn, bearing in mind that the consultant only had his experience of listening to the chest, before ultra sound, scans and echocardiograms were developed.

Often tricks would be played on junior nurses by the third years or new staff nurses. A favourite was to send a new nurse to another ward to collect a pair of fallopian tubes, or a long stand. This sometimes sounded plausible as we were often sent to other wards to borrow equipment. Another trick was to add orange squash to the test tube in the sluice. This would make it appear that the patient's urine was full of sugar. Urine was still tested at this time with tablets and droppers, with drops of urine into a test tube, often every four hours for unstable diabetics.

A lot of time was spent in the sluice during the first year. Crepe bandages were washed and reused, and stainless steel bedpans needed to be polished at the weekends. Later cardboard bedpans that fitted in a plastic mould were used and mashed up after use in a bedpan machine, which made life easier. Flower vases would get very stained and required attention, and soiled clothes need to be sluiced for relatives to take home.

Visiting hours were still quite strict in the 1960s and '70s. On Saturday and Sunday afternoons many visitors would arrive by car or bus and only two were allowed in for each patient. The others would wait in the League of Friends canteen. It would be an opportunity for staff to undertake the cleaning. This would be to clean and check suction and oxygen equipment. The drugs cupboard and trolley would be cleaned by the staff nurse and junior staff would clean cupboards in the sluice or equipment cupboards in the ward. Staff would note if any more bandages or pads were required to be ordered. The evening visiting was between 7.00 and 8.00 pm, which gave the nurse a chance to have a drink and write up the nurse's notes. Student nurses could also be tested on their surgical knowledge.

The idea of a coronary care unit was being bandied about. Stoke Mandeville's answer to this at the time was to make a room by the Sister's Office on the Men's Medical Ward available for a coronary bed. All the equipment such as monitors, defibrillators, oxygen, suction and a drug cabinet were installed. One patient in there arrested when I was on a lunch break in the middle of the night, but the first-year nurse I was on duty with had behaved surprisingly well, giving resuscitation and putting out the emergency call for the crash team.

Another time on that ward we nursed a young chap who had bright ginger hair. He had complications from German measles called Encephalitis. This is inflammation of the brain. When I returned after my day off, I could not see him on the ward. Had he died or been transferred to Oxford? No, shortly afterwards, I spotted a ginger haired chap pushing the tea trolley along the ward to help the staff. His quick recovery was amazing!

One evening I telephoned a nearby ward for some cheese for the other student and myself. We wanted to make some cheese on toast. Unfortunately, the night superintendent answered the telephone, so I quickly told him that a patient could not sleep and was hungry. Whether he believed me I do not know, but we got our cheese. Tea and toast were a great favourite for helping to get through the night.

Once every three months, a coach would be sent from the United States Air Force Base at Upper Heyford, as the Americans invited the Stoke Mandeville nurses to their socials. The only problem was that it left the front entrance at 6.30 pm just as the dining room was opening for our meal. My friend Rosalind and I would go into the dining room at 6.20 pm when most of the desserts would be laid ready and we would put cheese and biscuits into paper napkins to eat on the coach. The supper at the social consisted of hot dogs washed down with Coca Cola or cherryade. Alcohol was not served at all. Rosalind ended up marrying one of the servicemen she met at Upper Heyford, which did not please her parents very much.

Nurses served the meals so we learned a lot about special diets. If someone was given the wrong diet we would get into trouble. Often our butterfly hats got in the way of the curtains around the bed and would knock flowers and bowls from the locker.

Our starched hats were called butterfly hats and consisted of a long piece of cotton material and I always had a job to make them, though I was good at getting them stiff with the starch. I had plenty of practice by then with the St John hats and collars. I would starch the hats and two other girls took it in turns to make my hats up. I would place them on my dressing table, one to use and one as a spare in case of accidents on the ward. We kept them on with white Kirby hair grips.

Our mauve striped uniforms were quite tight at the waist and not very comfortable to wear. We were given eight starched aprons and after constant use the side of my arms would get quite sore from the movement against the apron. Each year a stripe was added to the dress on the left sleeve. The third year could not come fast enough. One of the advantages to living in the Nurses' Home was that there was always someone to help put rollers in, to set your hair for a date, and to borrow a handbag or a different top.

We were also expected to help the cleaner when she mopped one side of the ward. All the beds and lockers were moved to the other side then we helped move everything back. Beds were often moved up and down the ward, so if someone had the same surname, it was very important to ensure that you checked the wristband for the right patient. Each shift, a nurse would write something about the patient's treatment, care and condition in the Kardex. This was similar to index cards and made to fit inside a slim metal holder. Usually the doctor wrote in the medical notes. Nowadays it is all combined into a patient's notes and folders and often on a computer.

It was during my second year of night duty that I had my first driving lesson. At the time they were £1.2s.6d. a lesson and I had saved £60. Fortunately, I had an excellent teacher who was an examiner for the other driving instructors. I would have the lesson from 9.00 until 10.00 am after the night duty. The first lessons were all around the Southcourt estate opposite the hospital. My father took me out for practices when I was at home and I passed first time. No more waiting around for buses in the cold at Kingsbury Square. My parents gave me my mother's blue Morris Minor when she bought a more modern car and I now had freedom.

The typical Paediatric Surgical Ward would see toddlers confined to their cots in plaster of Paris, or on gallows traction for congenital dysplasia of the hips (clicky hips). The children would be on beds with traction for two to three months. Other cases would be boys with pyloric stenosis, where they had projectile vomiting and would require an operation on their stomach.

There were also the usual children that had appendicitis or injuries from a traffic accident. One such girl was Michele who was deeply unconscious from a road accident and needed full nursing care. She looked like a sleeping beauty lying on the bed with not a mark on her, but her brain must have been badly injured and I never heard if she was transferred to a neurological centre. It was on this ward that I removed sutures from a young patient as part of my practical final's exam. Another part of the practical was to care and clean a patient's tracheostomy tube. Part of the final practical exam was held in the School of Nursing at High Wycombe Hospital, and I remember that I was asked a lot of questions about diabetes and the care of the diabetic patient during the test.

On the Medical Children's Ward we had many babies come in with Gastroenteritis. These were very strictly nursed in cubicles. Another condition would be failure to thrive, which may have been because of infections, poor parenting, or bad home conditions such as mould and poor sanitation. Some babies had genetic faults and were abandoned by their parents. We were asked to make up specialist feeds for each patient's condition and Sister Vernon would write in the book what was required. Some had Carnation Milk in their feed and some had a mixture called Bengers Solution.

It was very hot in the milk kitchen, as we wore gowns and masks, and if we kept our hats on they would go limp with the steam from the sterilisers. I remember a very poorly baby on night duty whom an agency nurse was looking after and a message came through from the parents, to ask if the baby could be baptised before death, so the hospital admin contacted the chaplain. When he came to the ward, he requested a nurse to be in with him. As I was a practising Christian I went into the cubicle and joined in the prayers and responses.

Off duty, one of the activities that I enjoyed was taking part in the hospital shows. These were performed in the Nurses' Gymnasium and we had rehearsals two or three evenings per week. One of the clever medical staff wrote a pantomime on

Anadin and his Magic Clamp Pantomime

'Anadin and his Magic Clamp' as a skit on Aladdin. Some people dressed up as the doctors' hospital bleeps and I had a sister's part in one of the scenes. The other show was 'La Belle Helene' by Offenbach, when Rosalind and I had parts in the chorus.

Every December Sir Arthur Davis would bring his choir from Luton to give a concert in the gym. This was the famous Luton Girls' Choir. We would help push beds and wheelchairs down the long corridors so that the patients who were in the hospital a long time could enjoy the show. The corridors were said to be a quarter of a mile long, so we had quite a walk when going to the Nurses' Dining Room or League of Friends shop.

My gynaecological placement was a busy ward ruled over by Sister Butler. Many of the sisters still working at Stoke Mandeville had been nursing there since the war – they never married and were dedicated to their nursing. Unfortunately, at that time patients suffering a miscarriage were on the same ward as those that were having terminations. This proved upsetting at times. The 1967 Abortion Act allowed for terminations if there was a good reason and one girl I remember worked in the Central

Sterile Supply Department. She was only 17, unmarried and would not have been able to cope with a baby. Everything there was regimental, and many ladies were given salt baths to aid healing. The ward was spotlessly clean and the pre-op shaves were done to perfection. Sister Butler gave us a notebook to learn about the different types of hysterectomy, or about fibroids or prolapses. We learnt our surgery very well on that ward!

Another experience was working at a different hospital in the group, the Royal Buckinghamshire Hospital. Sir Harry Verney, the brother-in-law of Florence Nightingale, had involved her in the decision making when he was Member of Parliament for North Bucks. It is said that Florence Nightingale had a hand in its planning and design from 1856 onwards. It opened in1862 and Queen Victoria and the Rothchilds gave it their patronage. The hospital consisted of four long open wards and student nurses were sent to gain their orthopaedic experience there. I did not like this speciality much as it was heavy work and didn't seem to me to be very rewarding. The Women's Ward would be full of elderly ladies recovering from fractured femurs or, occasionally, tuberculosis of the bone, and the Male Ward tended to be busy with young men from road and motorbike accidents who acted very cheekily towards the staff. At this time, it also covered just two rooms set aside for accident and emergency.

Downstairs was the Maternity Department, where later in life I would have my two sons. On a lower ground floor was the outpatients clinic, which was very interesting. Not only did we get a chance to speak to the public, but the doctors would take time and trouble to explain conditions to the nurses. Preparing the patients for examinations and chaperoning were learned to support nervous patients. We also learnt how to make trays and trolleys for various procedures and had regular 8.00 am to 5.00 pm hours of duty. The special clinic for sexually transmitted diseases was down another flight of stairs. Students were not allowed in these clinics and they tended to be a little later after our shift. This was before the days of HIV/Aids, so most of the work was on venereal diseases and chlamydia infections.

It was during my student nurse days that I experienced my first ever package holiday to fly abroad. My friend Dorothy and I booked a five-day holiday to Malta, and the hot air rushed to my face as we stepped off the plane. I was hooked. The following year we went to Sorrento in Italy and I enjoyed the hotel waiters chatting to us. The third year we thought that we would try Blackpool for the night life, but it did not live up to our excitement and expectations... and it cost more than the holidays abroad!

Living in the Nurses' Home was very lively. The latest pop tunes of The Tremoloes, The Fortunes, The Walker Brothers, Herman's Hermits, Unit Four plus Two, Elvis and Cliff were among my favourites. Every Thursday evening the TV room would be packed, with standing room only, to hear the latest pop tunes and see what had moved in the charts. Another busy place would be by the telephone at the main door. We would queue to use the phone, or if it rang at other times we would take messages for nurses from their parents or boyfriends. The other form of communication was by letter – the pigeon hole by the entrance would be constantly checked for cards and love letters.

The final exam day arrived, when we sat two three-hour papers in the School of Nursing. The practical tests had all been completed and the hospital exams were over. This was now the finals for the State Registration.

A grand prize-giving ceremony was held in the Nurses' Gymnasium. A local florist provided all the plants around the stage for decoration and the Bucks Herald newspaper was in attendance. My parents arrived with Miss Amor, the Bletchley St John Superintendent. We lined up in our smartest uniforms

Presentation of
Certificates, Badges and Awards

at

STOKE MANDEVILLE HOSPITAL

WEDNESDAY, 10th NOVEMBER, 1971

at 6.30 p.m.

to receive our certificates and badges. Every nurse was very proud to be able to wear their hospital badge. At the Royal College of Nursing Headquarters in London they have a map of Britain formed by the hundreds of, now redundant, hospital badges. Stoke Mandeville's was the Florence Nightingale lamp, with the Royal Bucks and Associated Hospitals engraved around the side. Another bonus was that the lady presenting the awards was our County Superintendent of Buckinghamshire St John Ambulance, Mrs Margaret Boothman who knew me from my cadet days. I felt very proud as I stood there after all my hard work...

Like many nurses, I still have the souvenirs from my nursing days – the lovely silver buckle attached to the navy Petersham Belt, the name badges, fob watch, nurses' scissors and an engraved silver Parker pen presented to me when I left the ward. Uniforms have been replaced with scrubs outfits with the name often embroidered on the chest. These were more comfortable and easily laundered, but the smartness and professionalism of the old styles were important for discipline and efficiency years ago.

CHAPTER 8
NURSING – A PASSION

After I qualified, I got my wish to return to Ward 9 to be a Staff Nurse. Jean Taylor was the more experienced Staff Nurse and we had two State Enrolled Nurses. Students at that time made up the workload and a lot of time and effort went into training them about surgical nursing. The two main surgeons were Mr Hadfield and Mr Pryer, and the ward was very busy with many men from mid and north Bucks coming for operations. Sister Godwin's Ward 10 would be 'on take' one week and Robin Radley's Ward 9, my ward, the next.

We would bring the patients back from theatre with their airway in and 'special' them at the bedside until fully recovered. Once their blood pressure was stable, we would gradually sit them up, give them a wash and freshen up and offer a mouth wash. Good post-op care included having everything ready at the bedside that could be required. An oxygen cylinder was by the bed and a suction unit on a chair, as it was not piped into the ward in those days. Bed packs, catheter bags, drip stands etc would all be ready for the post-op patient.

In hindsight I should have stayed at Stoke Mandeville, but in those days it was expected that you would move on after six months staffing to undertake more training. During the latter part of 1972, I undertook the short psychiatric nursing course at St John's Hospital, Stone (the old asylum), just outside the town. The psychology and diseases of the brain fascinated me and I spent a very enjoyable time there. I sampled a long-stay ward and the Acute Nervous Breakdown Ward. We were given regular training days and seminars.

The food at the hospital was excellent and it had its own bakery and orchard. Staff and patients alike enjoyed dances in the entertainment's hall on Thursday evenings, given by the hospital's band. The hospital had its own shop, fire station, occupational therapy and work shop. It was a community in itself and conditions for staff were very good.

As I was a qualified nurse, I was given a large bedsit and my own bathroom in the modern Whittingham House. Even though I had my car, I could catch the bus straight into Aylesbury or go the other way and explore Thame.

Mr Peters, the Director of Nursing, was very keen to retain staff and said if I wanted to come back later on, he would be very pleased to have me. This proved prophetic! I had met Paul when he was on one of the wards at Stoke Mandeville and I visited him in Northampton when he was discharged, so it was to Northampton that I applied to undertake Midwifery training.

This proved to be a big mistake as the Barrett Maternity Home had nearly five thousand deliveries a year and it felt to me to be just mass production. As soon as a mother had delivered, all they wanted to do, naturally, was to go home with their baby. I did not get the job satisfaction of nursing a patient that I had had in general nursing. At times it was pandemonium, with women having babies everywhere. Some arrived in a taxi just about to deliver; others might be in the waiting room, and one even delivered in a corridor.

One day I was walking along a corridor when I saw smoke coming out of a sluice room, and on further examination I saw that a bin on the floor had caught fire, a mother having gone into the sluice for a crafty smoke. A porter was nearby, so I grabbed him and we got the bin into the sink and poured water into it or the old building could easily have had a nasty fire.

Looking back, the best parts of that time were actually delivering 70 babies under the supervision of a qualified midwife and my placement at the Ante-Natal Clinic. So many different mothers from all around Northampton came for examination and advice and I was much more suited to community work! This was before regular scans were in operation.

One day a Cyclops baby was born. This is a congenital deformity when there is just one eye formed in the middle of the forehead and all the nursing staff were asked to see the baby for our education. The baby had some other deformities not compatible with life, so it was wrapped up and kept warm until it faded away. Even children born with some heart deformities could not be operated on or saved in those days.

The conditions for pupil midwives were not very good. Although we were qualified nurses, we were not even allowed to give a Paracetamol tablet. Many of the midwives were ageing spinsters and were not to my liking. The rebel had had enough. I left midwifery and joined a Nurses' Agency for three months to see if I could settle in Northampton. I was given a placement in a convalescent home, which I really enjoyed as this was leading up to the Christmas celebrations of 1973. But Northampton was not for me. It was too big and industrial and I wanted to go back to Aylesbury where I had been so happy.

It was so strange, because I had gone away and returned, but I was thought more of than if I had stayed at Stoke Mandeville. There was a chronic shortage of nurses at that time and one could have the pick of the jobs. Because the pay was so bad, managers got around this for qualified nurses by making the staff nurses junior sisters, so I managed to go back to Ward 9.

There were not many male general nurses at that time, though there were more male nurses in Mental Health and I think they were teased quite a bit to be nursing. The Night Superintendent was a qualified paediatric nurse, but like many others he went into senior administration work later on. Part-time nurses were also discriminated against a little as they wore a pink dress under their apron, not the pale blue like the full-time staff.

A lot of this altered in 1974 when there were huge demonstrations about pay and conditions and the NHS underwent a reorganisation. Nurses would be given a proper salary and be encouraged to live out. They would be given lockers for their uniforms so they could change before work. Staff would pay for meals in the dining room and their salary was administered by cheque into their bank account. Many more procedures were developed to be carried out in the outpatients departments and a special day case ward was established. It was a time when many changes were taking place in hospitals. New wards would be in four- and six-bedded bays. More equipment would be used from the Central Sterile Supply Department and recovery areas in theatre were established. Patient centred care became the norm with nurses responsible for a set number of patients instead of sharing all the workload from a workbook. Intravenous infusions had changed from being given from a bottle to plastic bags; syringes were disposable and diabetic tests could be carried out with dipsticks instead of the time-consuming tablets with test tubes. Evidenced based practice was in fashion, with nurses encouraged to ask why something was being carried out, as it had been for many years. Reflective practice sessions were introduced to look at what had been done and if procedures could be improved.

One way to become a sister in my own right was to go onto night duty. This involved permanent nights, not a rotation system as it is now, and there were a lot of permanent night staff. I would work eight nights on duty and six nights off. We started at 8.30 pm and finished at 7.30 am, with an hour's lunch break at 11.00 pm or at twelve midnight. I was given eight wards to look after, including the two children's wards, the Gynaecological Ward, an Acute Elderly Ward and Ward 15, the private patients' ward. I would visit each ward at 10.00 pm,

2.00 am and 6.00 am. Staff would be expected to report to me on the most seriously ill patients and their care.

Staff on the surgical wards were kept busy at night changing catheter bags and adding up the fluid charts. On post-operative patients it was very important that they checked the wound site for bleeding and constantly checked that the intravenous infusions were dripping at the correct rate. Observations throughout the night on patients having a blood transfusion were essential as they could deteriorate and suffer a reaction.

Night time was also an opportunity to undertake some teaching sessions with the student nurses. Sometimes a student would want to take one of their final assessments on night duty and I enjoyed participating in their learning.

We tried not to call the House Doctor out to the ward unless it was absolutely necessary. They had been working and on call for many hours and badly required their sleep. I would confirm any expected deaths on the elderly ward and take a verbal message for medication if required. The doctor would be bleeped if a patient suddenly deteriorated or if an emergency admission was arriving.

This job proved to be very interesting with lots of variety. I would be taking emergency admissions to theatre and bringing them back later in the night. Another duty would be to fetch blood packs from the path lab for the overnight blood transfusions, then double checking them with the nurse in charge of the ward. It was creepy going to the back of the hospital in the middle of the night – the cockroaches would be crawling across the back corridor and sometimes the hospital cats would be prowling around! I would also spend time with the relatives of very sick patients and sometimes have the sad duty of informing relatives that their loved one had passed away during the night.

One night we had the emergency admission of a young girl with a suspected ruptured ectopic pregnancy. This is when the egg develops along the fallopian tube instead of planting into the uterus. If it ruptures, the patient may die of peritonitis. The girl was brought in very shocked and taken straight on the admission trolley to theatre. The amazing thing that sticks in my memory is that her GP came along in the ambulance with her and, holding her hand, escorted her to theatre in the middle of the night.

It wasn't all happy endings. One morning a man recovering from having his kidney removed started to become breathless – he had developed a pulmonary embolism. The doctors did what they could for him with drugs and oxygen but all we could do was hold his hand until, sadly, he passed away before his relatives arrived. These were the days before clot busting drugs or putting someone into a medically induced coma.

If there was a cardiac arrest at night the senior staff would all be bleeped and expected to rush and lend a hand on the ward. The sisters on the medical side would be expected to push the cardiac trolley from a central room to the correct ward, as each ward did not have its own defibrillator and resus drugs in those days.

Another night I remember was when a post-operative man became very confused, as his electrolytes were imbalanced and he got out of bed and was hallucinating. He managed to barricade himself into the treatment room and started throwing packs and bottles around. Eventually the Night Superintendent, who was a male nurse, and myself managed to restrain him and he was given a dose of Paraldehyde to sedate him, which was the procedure in those days for such emergencies.

One Saturday night we received some casualties suffering from food poisoning due to the food buffet having been left around the hall far too long, from the afternoon meal and on to the evening party. Some guests were taken to the medical wards, but one lady proved to be very ill and I was selected to travel with her to the Slade Hospital in Oxford where she could have specialist care.

If the opposite sister was coming on duty on my last night, sometimes the Night Superintendent would let the first sister off, halfway through the night at 2.00 am, for the new sister to take over. This was often done if the sister felt ill or was going off on holiday, or if the weather was bad.

Night duty enabled me to purchase many of the items Paul and I needed to equip our house. We had a modern terraced house on Bedgrove and were able to purchase furniture for the bedrooms, a modern television, music centre and save up for holidays.

Eighteen months was enough. I had got trapped on night duty and it was time to try something else. A career in nursing can be so varied as it gives the opportunity to study, to specialise in many areas, or work in the community, departments or wards. I went back to undertake psychiatric nurse training at St John's Hospital in 1976 and did not look back.

CHAPTER 9
MENTAL HEALTH TRAINING

Mental health work was changing. During the 1950s many new drugs had become available so more people could be cared for at home. The old fence and gates around the 'County Asylum' had been removed and most of the patients were there as voluntary patients. The number of in-patients went down from its peak of 1,000 in the 1950s to between 400-500 during the 1970s.

I could train in 18 months as I already had my general nursing qualification, and without loss of pay, thanks to the unions that had negotiated to encourage staff to undertake more training! The training was more relaxed than in general nursing and the classrooms in the small school of nursing were very pleasant, overlooking the Chiltern Hills. As there were only two of us doing the shortened training, we joined other small sets and gradually came to know the workings of the hospital.

I suppose the main difference working there was that we did not wear uniforms. Individual styles to a certain extent were encouraged, as long as the clothes didn't make you vulnerable with safety. Some staff with long hair and scruffy clothes made it difficult, on the acute ward, to distinguish the staff from the patients. There was more male staff than female, which I did not mind as it was a much nicer atmosphere than with the staff in the maternity hospital.

I found work on the chronic wards easy as the pace was so slow and many patients had been there for years and more or less ran the ward. We were required to undertake a case study of a person who had been at the hospital a long time. This would be to examine why they had been admitted and what the possible plans were for them to be cared for elsewhere.

Acute work was different. I was placed on a ward for men specifically suffering from depression and personality disorders, and you needed your wits about you to closely observe them. Some men were very quiet and withdrawn and others were extrovert and very lively. Some were manipulative and others demanding – this was a real test for the staff. Teamwork was essential so that all the staff were working to the same model and procedures.

I remember one unusual case of a man suffering from amnesia. This stress in his life had made him completely shut down and his brain could not function with recent events. With tender loving care and support, he was able, after a couple of months, to gradually resume his life without constant monitoring. Another man had a lot to say for himself and was suffering from a bipolar behavioural condition. When he was high, he would attend the Thursday night social in the entertainments hall and helped me learn some dances, but when he was low, he needed to be coaxed to get out of bed and wash himself. (The hospital had its own band led by the senior nurse, Mr Snooks, playing the violin.) We were required to undertake a study of different interventions used, and later an assessment on running the ward and organising a group of patients.

I was often asked to help with Electric Convulsive Therapy because of my previous general nurse training and experience at Stoke Mandeville. This could be from accompanying the patient in the minibus over to the ECT Unit in Beacon House or helping check and prepare the equipment and assisting the doctors. One day I was accompanying a lady in the minibus for ECT and she suddenly hit me on the nose with her fist and made my nose bleed. It was my fault really, as I had got too close to her and invaded her personal space. She was probably anxious about having ECT and wanted to take it out on someone in authority.

There was much outcry over the years about ECT, stating that the treatment was barbaric, but I did witness how patients improved slowly afterwards, especially if they had been so depressed that they would not eat or drink. It could be a life saver and was not given before medication and talking therapies had been first tried. Usually two electrodes would be placed over either one or both sides of the temple and an electric current passed through. The patient was fully anaesthetised first and it only lasted a short time, similar to going for a tooth extraction at the dentist! I found care in the recovery room and gradually orientating the patients afterwards very rewarding.

Beacon House was the unit where people were placed who had had a nervous breakdown. It was modern and had separate men's and women's sections. Some patients were placed in a seclusion room for their own good and would have their own special nurse on a one to one basis. The room was very basic with just a mattress on the floor and no personal belongings, to remove the temptation of self-harming. Sometimes we would have people with drug addictions and other times patients would need to be transferred to specialist units for drug dependency or forensic psychiatry.

My placements included experience in the Occupational Therapy Department and the Industrial Unit. Here many patients would do assembly work for local firms and packing, like sheltered employment. I believe at one time they packed Readers Digest Magazines. One week I accompanied patients to Askeys, a local firm making ice cream wafers, and worked with the patients to see how they coped with work outside the hospital. We could always purchase beautiful fresh rolls from the hospital bakery and take patients to the shop for a coffee. We could also accompany patients to the chapel for the service on a Sunday or take them for a walk in the orchard. It was a self-contained community and I enjoyed working within it. In the print shop they printed many programmes, tickets and leaflets for local groups which supported the local community.

There was always plenty of overtime available if one wanted it. I remember Howard Ward, full of ladies who had been there for twenty years or more. It was their home, very pretty with lace curtains around the rooms and pretty bedspreads. Some of these ladies went to group homes and elderly care homes later on, but in the 1970s it was their refuge.

My night duty included three weeks on the (then called) Psycho Geriatric Ward. Most of the patients would sleep, but there was always the odd one that would want to wander 'to go to work' or 'walk home'. The Night Superintendent, Mr Brewster, gave me quite a shock one night, when he crept into the ward as he was a very black man and suddenly appeared like a ghost.

The day sister here was obsessional about the patients' bowels and would often give them weekly enemas, as she had probably had a patient with a blockage that developed peritonitis. We now know that regular purgatives make the rectal muscles sluggish and less able to perform. Woe betide the nurse that gave too many enemas at once – there would not be enough toilets for the desperate patients and commodes would be hastily brought in!

During the training we were taken to Grendon Underwood Prison for the day. This was to introduce us to groups and group therapy work. Grendon Underwood had pioneered a scheme to enable suitable prisoners to discuss their problems in an open forum. We were locked in and experienced a day in the life of a prisoner. The other trip from the training school that year was to the Ley Clinic in Oxford. Here we learned about many different addictions, e.g. drug, alcohol and food.

After the hospital finals and having passed the practical assignment it was time for the RMN examination. This consisted of two three-hour written papers. One of the questions was a First Aid-type question about bleeding and self-harm, so I think this must have helped me get through. I just managed to take the exams before I went off on maternity leave as I was seven months pregnant with my first son then. At that time, we were given ten weeks before the birth and eight weeks afterwards on full pay as maternity entitlement. If you wanted more maternity leave it was six months half pay and that was it. I did not want to manage on half pay, so after using my annual leave entitlement I went back to work, when Matthew was ten weeks old. It worked out surprisingly well!

The prize-giving ceremony had changed since my general nursing and the presentations were now taking place in the Stoke Mandeville Sports and Social Club. The event was being modernised and we all wore mufti. Roger Titley came over for the photographs with me and my parents, as he was my St John President. A buffet then followed. The VIP who gave the presentations and speeches reminded nurses to always keep the 'human touch' as this was vital for a career in nursing!

RMN Prize-giving with my tutor, John Jonas, and my parents, Feb 1978

Part 2

CHAPTER 10
FAMILY LIFE 1974-2000

Paul and I were married on 24th August 1974 at St Martin's Church, Fenny Stratford. This was the church where my family had always worshipped. I was christened and confirmed there and had been a Sunday School teacher.

The wedding reception was held in St Martin's Hall. This was a bit of a disappointment, as we had hoped to hold a small reception in The Bletchley Arms Hotel, but St Martin's Hall was more affordable. Mum and Dad wanted to invite a lot of friends and family, so tried to organise the day. Mum played her electric organ for some dancing and Uncle Tom tried to run a

The Pacey Clan at my wedding

Six Pacey children, August 1974

bar. My parents told the caterers the wrong time for the meal, not realising how long photographs and meeting the guests would take. This was before the idea of evening parties. They had more idea for my sister's wedding in 1977. For Rosemary's wedding they organised a proper bar and the catering arrangements were much improved!

After my wedding, I changed at Auntie Gert's house and we left them all to it and early evening set off for The Randolph Hotel, Oxford for a short honeymoon. It was the August Bank Holiday weekend and we spent the next three nights at a boutique hotel in Ross-on-Wye.

Paul got a job with the Aylesbury hospitals as a plumber and maintenance engineer, which proved interesting, as he visited all three hospitals in the group to assist with repairs. Later he became a Planner Estimator based at Stoke Mandeville, cycling to work, so we only needed one car.

Our first home in married life was in Lancaster Road, Aylesbury. This was a modern mid-terraced house, on a large private estate called Bedgrove. Christine and Maurice Washington, our neighbours, lived at number 9. They would go on to have two boys the same age as ours and they played together. We still keep in touch with them now. On the other side of our house (at number 5) lived Joyce and Ken Stent. They had two girls that were slightly older.

I got to know many of the neighbours in those days because it became the fashion to hold Tupperware and Avon parties. Not many of these ladies worked, or, if they did, it was part-time. I spent a few evenings having a laugh with the ladies at dress parties. Children would happily play on the green opposite, where the mothers had a good view of them, as the kitchens were in the front of the house.

Like everywhere else in the 1970s and '80s people gradually had double glazing and central heating installed, and front porches built. I remember that our porch was built over the weekend of Prince Charles and Lady Diana's wedding and we had a celebration and lunch in the back garden. On another occasion when a Lancaster Road street party was being held, I remember having to leave early for night duty.

I used the launderette around the corner at the Bedgrove shops for three months after we got married until Paul plumbed in a front-loading automatic washing machine. Instead of using cash at Budgens, gradually a bank card took over. Salaries were not great in those days, so if we both worked full-time hours we could run a car, pay the bills and have two weeks holiday each year. The only way we could change our car was to have a loan. After the old Morris Minor, we had a second-hand Volkswagen Golf. The house had electric storage heaters, which were expensive to run and we should have changed to central heating, but we did not want the upset that would be involved with replacing the carpets and redecorating.

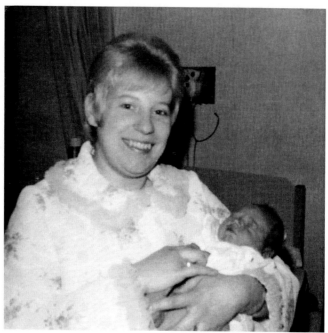

With Matthew on Christmas Eve 1977

My first child, Matthew, arrived in December 1977, four days before Christmas. Matthew, means 'gift from God'. I stayed in The Royal Bucks Hospital over Christmas, so I did not have to worry about meals and visitors. In those days one could stay in for up to five days! Hazel and Nigel had Paul for a Christmas meal and the other days he came to the ward.

Matthew was an easy baby and slept very well, so well I had to constantly check that he was OK. We soon settled into a routine and I was able to go back to work at St John's Hospital, Stone, when he was ten weeks old.

I was sent to work on Willow Ward because of my general training. This was the sick bay for anyone ill at the hospital. Patients mainly came from the long-stay wards with leg ulcers, pressure sores, chest infections, unstable diabetes, or to convalesce from a stay at Stoke Mandeville. The ward had been recently modernised and was only ten beds and a day room. This was my first experience using a hoist for lifting patients from both the beds and baths. It helped save the nurses' backs, which could be damaged with a lot of heavy lifting. Years ago, 40,000 nurses were reporting back related injuries annually.

The old method of egg white and oxygen to use on bedsores proved effective on the ward, as egg white is protein and oxygen is good for cells, so it made some sense. Nowadays there are specialised pressure mattresses and many types of dressings for pressure sores and skin ulcers.

I worked opposite another general trained staff nurse and we had a male State Enrolled Nurse called Harry. This all worked in my favour as Harry wanted as many extra shifts as possible as he was saving up to get a mortgage with his beloved girlfriend Susie. If I wanted to swap a shift then Harry would oblige. I would try to swap with Harry for the St John meetings where I volunteered.

We always kept a notebook in our pocket for the handover. This was very useful for tips and advice passed on from the previous shift. Sometimes we would forget to hand over the keys for the ward and the medicine cupboard, only to discover them in the pocket of the uniform on reaching home. You would be required to trail all the way back to the ward to hand them back!

In 1978 Willow Ward was the showpiece of the hospital and was presented with the first colour television set that came to the hospital. The local Rotary Club wanted to support the hospital and convey to the public that mental health was an illness that anyone could suffer from.

This was the start of modernising the hospital, but the writing was on the wall and big changes soon took place. The hospital would close completely in 1992. A large garden party was held in the grounds of St John's Hospital to celebrate, and staff family and friends were all invited. The emphasis was to be on 'Care in

First Colour TV – Presentation to Willow Ward by Rotary

1853 — 1991   *VAL.*

AYLESBURY VALE HEALTH AUTHORITY

You, your partner and your children are invited to

A CELEBRATION OF ST. JOHN'S HOSPITAL

on

SATURDAY 7th SEPTEMBER 1991

12 noon – 5 p.m.

TO MARK THE CLOSURE OF THE HOSPITAL

CLOSING CEREMONY 4 p.m.

Barbeque Lunch 1 p.m.   Tea 3.30 p.m.
Small Display of the Hospital of the 1920's/1930's

PTO

the Community', which involved group homes, specialised units and expansion of community nursing services.

The only drawback of working there was that I had lost my protected salary from being a student and was on part-time staff nurses' money. I worked thirty hours a week, which just meant that I did not work the long day shifts. The shifts were quite good as we had every other weekend off, and on the following week we had days off in the week. This meant that Paul had the baby at the weekend and I enjoyed days off during the week when everyone else was at work and we only needed the childminder four days a week.

Another drawback was that Willow Ward was by the mortuary and could be quite creepy at night, but there were not many deaths at the hospital! Most of the work was in the morning, washing and dressing patients, or doing treatments and dressings. The patients enjoyed the day room, reading, or watching the television, and some of their friends from around the hospital would come to visit. This worked well until the middle of the next winter.

It was no joke trying to take Matthew to the childminder at 6.30 am to be on duty for 7 o'clock. I needed to look for another job with better hours.

As he got older, the childminder took Matthew to the playgroup that she went to. My midwife used this childminder and she told me about St Francis de Sales preparatory school at Tring, where her son was going. This helped me a great deal as they took boys from three years and were excellent with learning and playing.

When Matthew was 6 years old, he joined the junior branch of St John Ambulance Cadets and became one of the first children to join the new Badger group, as it was called. Paul and I did lots of activities with the group to enable them to work for the Super Badger Award, but Paul would run the Badger set on his own when I moved to lead the Adult Division. Matthew enjoyed going to the local Beaver group, part of the Scouts situated on

Our family in 1979

Bedgrove at Dover Hedge, so we made lots of friends locally. When Matthew was 8, he started to learn the violin, which pleased Grandma Pacey. He got on very well with the violin teacher who lived opposite us.

We saved up each year and had some wonderful holidays abroad. One year we visited Malta, another year Corfu and also Torremolinos, Spain and Tunisia. The year before Stephen was born, we had a lovely holiday to Cyprus.

Stephen, meaning 'crowned one', was born at Easter 1983 and again settled easily into a routine. Stephen was christened on 10th July that year, on a very hot summer's day. Matthew had been christened on a cold February day at The Church of the Holy Spirit, Bedgrove, and went to Sunday School there, but Stephen could not be christened at Bedgrove Church because of summer holidays. Mum was so pleased when it was arranged for him to be christened where she was the organist at All Saints Church,

Stephen's Christening at All Saints, Soulbury, 10th July 1983

111

Soulbury. Peter Lymbery, our old St John Superintendent was Church Warden and Rev Paul Drake officiated.

When we arrived back at the house for lunch, it was so hot I immediately changed into a sundress and several umbrellas were placed around the garden for all the aunties. Aunties Beat, Nora, Alice and Gert, plus the grandparents were all in attendance. By then I was a Community Psychiatric Nurse and worked very closely with Social Services. They all wanted to see the new baby at the Social Services Office in town, so that was my project whilst on leave, to show him to my Social Services colleagues and to the members of the day clubs.

One of the ladies who had two daughters attending St Francis de Sales School became Stephen's childminder. I would take her daughters to school with Matthew and she would take Stephen home. I could do the morning runs, providing the other mums could cover the afternoons. The childminders were all registered with Social Services, so when I needed to find another childminder, they obliged by telling me about the childminders on Elmhurst Estate. Auntie Dee and Auntie Sue ran the Elmhurst playgroup, so this worked well before Stephen went on to the school in Tring, just as Matthew had done. Stephen had some lovely parts in school plays, especially at Christmas. He was an angel, a coot bird one year, a shepherd boy another and an old lady another. Attending the school shows was a must.

Our worst holiday was in 1984, when we had decided to spend two weeks on the Isle of Wight. The first week was in a bed and breakfast at Ryde, as we did not know that side of the island. The second week was at the St John Ambulance County Cadet Camp. Unbelievably, it rained the whole two weeks, every day. It cost more, going shopping and finding activities to do and we did not feel that we had a break. After that I made sure that we always had a least one week abroad for the sunshine.

Stephen followed Matthew's lead by joining the Badgers and Beavers and enjoyed the many physical activities on offer –

Stephen's 5 Birthday Party in the church hall

swimming lessons, learning to ride a bicycle and gym classes. He was livelier than Matthew and had a job to concentrate. Boys do not like academic work much, so I would listen to him reading outside the school each morning when he was more awake and this seemed to work.

When Stephen was 6 years old, we moved to a bigger house on the other side of the estate. It had lovely recreational paths and was near the park, but I think they missed playing with their friends around the green.

Both boys enjoyed the Scouts (4th Aylesbury Branch) and fondly remember a leader called Postie who was fantastic with boys, a real role model. He told them wonderful stories and encouraged them to sing songs around the campfire. They went on lovely camps and both did expeditions to gain the Chief Scouts Award. The boys worked hard to gain their Grand Prior's Badge at St John and I remember them organising a concert to perform to the elderly at Long Crendon Day Club.

One year the violin teacher helped Matthew organise some musical items to entertain the parents at the cadet presentation evening. Both boys went to the County St John Camp each year at Stoats Farm, Totland Bay. Stephen continued as an adult to go on the advance party to help get the camp ready for the Cadets in its new home in Charmouth, Dorset.

Matthew was selected to be the Lord Lieutenant's St John Cadet for 1993. This was a great honour and involved accompanying the Lord Lieutenant when members of the Royal Family came to Buckinghamshire. It was usually to open a hospital ward, a headquarters, shopping centre or adventure playground. I accompanied Matthew as his guardian and chauffeur and we were usually briefed a few days before. The arrangements had to be kept very confidential because of security issues. Matthew met HRH Princess Anne, HRH Prince Andrew, The Duchess of Gloucester and the Duchess of Kent that year.

In 1996 St John held a competition to encourage groups to use publicity to showcase their divisions. Matthew and I entered, with a magazine showing how our group recruited and held events. We won this competition and were awarded a medallion called the Merritt Award for PR (Public Relations).

Instead of giving health professionals more money, the Government kept giving extra days holiday. This suited me as we had all the Bank Holidays and I was fortunate to be able to spread my holiday leave to include the school half terms too. The typical week's holiday would be to have three days at home to catch up on house jobs, whilst the boys played with their friends or attended a holiday sports course. We would then have three days out with one being a day at Milton Keynes shops and the cinema. Another would be a visit to London, very often to the large museums, and the final day would be a trip out in the car, depending on the weather. We would often take Auntie Kit on these trips as she relied on buses to go anywhere. On Bank Holidays we would have everything packed and get away as early as possible, to have three or four days' bed and breakfast at different venues around the country, such as Margate, Weston-super-Mare, Great Yarmouth, Bournemouth, Paignton, Brighton, Hastings and Dover – all were visited during the 1980s.

Paul and I split up in 1989 and both went our separate ways. I moved with the boys to Howard Avenue, just around the corner from our first house in Lancaster Road. Paul took digs until he was able to purchase his house in Redland Way. The boys would stay with him on alternate weekends and go for tea one evening a week. The weekends that I did not have the boys, I would do a shift at Chiltern View Nursing Home at Stone. It also allowed me to get jobs done in the home. I let the garage to a local man who wanted to store his antique Jaguar car and found a handyman to decorate the house. Brian Mountain, a local plumber from church, put in a new power shower and upgraded the central heating. Over the years we had new double glazing, the loft boarded with sockets, switches installed and a summer house that the boys loved to play in.

The boys were fortunate to be able to go to the Aylesbury Music Centre on Saturday mornings. It improved their violin playing and gave them experience at performing with others. Matthew played in a concert in the grounds of Stowe School, and Stephen played the drums and percussion instruments at Waddesdon Manor.

Stephen has recently reminded me of the time we went to the Birmingham Motor Show, when we had a lovely day sitting in all the posh cars. Unfortunately, we did not have any photographs to prove it, as we discovered on returning home that there was not a film in the camera!

We enjoyed some stays at Center Parcs, and for my fortieth birthday had a break to the Sherwood Forest resort near Nottingham. Rosemary and family came to join us as day visitors, which was lovely. One year we were at Center Parcs and it clashed with Matthew having to perform a duty as the Lord Lieutenant's Cadet, so we came all the way back along the M1 motorway during the afternoon, went to the evening ceremony and travelled back that night to the resort!

Matthew was able to transfer to Aylesbury Grammar School when he was 12 years old. He went for an interview and test and it was agreed that he could go there provided he retook the first senior year again. Stephen by this time was at Broughton Junior School and one of my St John ladies, Janet Holden, looked for him coming out of school.

Stephen achieved his Chief Scout Challenge with three Scout friends after his expedition in the Lake District, National Park. He also progressed well in the St John Cadets and had the honour of representing the Buckinghamshire Cadets at a reception held at Buckingham Palace during 1998. This was hosted by HRH Princess Anne, Commandant in Chief of Cadets.

I enjoyed my years working on the bank rota, nursing at Chiltern View. This was a 30-bedded home for people with advanced dementia. Usually they could not be managed at other homes and needed the expertise of Registered Mental Nurses and skilled care assistants. I would work an afternoon shift once a fortnight, but later on managed a night shift once a fortnight on a Friday night. The home was built with two wings and was all on the flat. Each patient had their own room and wash basin. Some would sleep well all night, whereas others would be up and wandering up and down the corridors. As dawn approached, especially in the summer months, it was lovely to go out in the garden and watch the sunrise over the hills. It was opened by HRH The Duchess of Gloucester, accompanied by The Rt Hon William Whitelaw, who was on the Brendoncare Board at the time.

As there was a singles club meeting at the Plough Public House, Tring Road, I went along one evening to see what they did. It was here that I met John in February 1992 and we started going out to events together. John was single and his mother had died a few years before. We had many short breaks and days out, finally deciding to get married in 1999. Pooling our money from the two houses, we bought a house in Herston Close, Bedgrove, as we wanted something different for our life together. We didn't want to embarrass the boys and there's so much choice now for wedding venues, so we decided to have a tropical wedding in Kenya, and on our return we would have a family party to celebrate. Another chapter in the life of the rebel had begun.

After getting the appropriate paperwork, we arrived at Turtle Beach Resort near Mombasa. The first week was spent relaxing and acclimatising. We enjoyed a two-night tented safari to East Tsavo National Park to see the big five African animals. We enjoyed a meal around the campfire and an early rise to spot animals around the water hole. Another outing was to visit the Portuguese sites in Mombasa and visit a school, where we took some materials.

A lady named Nancy was our wedding planner. The choices on offer were varied. I chose a large flower bouquet of white flowers, roses and frangipanis to match my dress. We had the local Baptist Choir singing Swahili choruses and chants, and a group of Masa Mari warriors leading our wedding procession. A registrar came out from Mombasa to conduct the ceremony in the beautiful tropical garden. Much of what he said was about bigamy! After the procession around the flower petal strewn garden, we had more photographs on the beach.

The wedding was held at 4.00 pm when the weather was getting a little cooler, and the wedding party at 5 o'clock in a summer house. This included some holiday makers that acted as bridesmaid, best man and witnesses. Our cake was iced with a red heart shape and the whole thing was videoed. During the evening we enjoyed the dancing, hotel band and entertainment. A full wedding breakfast was included on the terrace the next

Our wedding in Kenya, 12th October 1999

morning. The wedding cost £500 on top of the two weeks holiday cost, and we are on their wedding board of honour!

On the Friday after our return, a wedding party was held at the Aylesbury Holiday Inn. The Rev David Nash performed the wedding blessing and Dave Moore was the best man. John's friend, Phil Morrell, videoed this for us and another friend, Phil Hawkins, provided the music. Sandy, my CPN (Community Psychiatric Nurse) colleague, decorated the room and secretary Janice Embury made the cake. It was lovely that John's elderly Aunt Elsie and my mother and Auntie Gert were able to attend. Rosemary and her family came with many friends from St John, the clubs and work.

Both boys went on Easter revision courses to help them gain good grades in their GCSEs, and Matthew wanted to gain his A Levels in order to go to University to train as a teacher. Stephen settled down and transferred to the sixth form of the John Colet School in Wendover and pursued a course in Tourism and Business Studies. He had a choice of going to Plymouth, or Bournemouth Universities. He chose Bournemouth for the beautiful beaches and university status, as it ranked number one for his chosen course. Matthew had a choice of Lancaster or Nottingham and chose Nottingham. Matthew could come home on the National Express bus to the coach station at Milton Keynes, where I would collect him in the car. Later on, Stephen would travel on the Stagecoach to Oxford Coach Station.

Another milestone was having driving lessons. There was an elderly instructor locally who was excellent with the teenagers on Bedgrove, and he enabled them to both pass their test. Stephen passed the first time and Matthew the second time, when they were 17. Another skill and another box ticked!

Both boys had a four-year university course. Matthew's course involved a year's teaching practice at different types of primary schools, some in wealthy areas and others in deprived areas. He graduated with a First-Class Honours Degree and advanced teaching status, which has enabled him to teach in many schools around the world. Stephen gained hotel experience at a five-star hotel in central London, which was part of the Red Carnation Group – he gained valuable customer experience at the concierge desk. He qualified in business and tourism and started work with Bournemouth Tourism. He later learned lifesaving skills, and became a First Aid trainer and personal trainer with the New Forest Council. Another ambition of his was to work at Center Parcs, and this he achieved when he gained a job at the new Woburn Forest site. Later, an opportunity arose for Stephen to train in the Fire Service. This was also an ambition from his childhood, and in 2018 he was accepted into the Bedfordshire Fire Service. Another chapter had begun.

CHAPTER 11
MY ST JOHN LIFE

Looking back, I feel that I have had three lives. One was my nursing career, the second a full family life and the third, a long career with St John Ambulance. This was to be from 1958 until 2013.

It all started when I spotted a girl at school wearing a red badge with a white cross on it. I asked her what it was for and she said that she was a member of the Bletchley St John Cadets. She told me that they met every Wednesday evening and learned First Aid and bandaging. My ears pricked up; this might be just what I needed to help me to go nursing.

The next Wednesday my mother took me along to the child welfare clinic where the meeting was held. I met Miss Day who had run the division since it was formed in 1942. She was ably assisted by Mrs Gladys Walpole, a very active, talented woman who had returned to help following the birth of her three children. The junior section was for girls aged 8 to 11 years.

We learned the many uses of the triangular bandage, how to treat nose bleeds, how to prepare and serve an invalid tray and how to wrap a parcel correctly, among other useful jobs. We would have an active game and often be practising for a concert to perform to the parents.

I did not know it at the time, but my grandfather's cousin, Mrs Emily Brooks, left money to the Bletchley St John Ambulance which formed most of the money that enabled St John to build the headquarters in Sherwood Drive opposite

Necessary Qualifications of a First Aider

In order to render the skilled assistance required, the First Aider should be:

a) **Observant,** that he may note the causes and signs of injury.

b) **Tactful,** that he may without thoughtless questions, learn the symptoms and history of the case, and secure the confidence of the patient and bystanders

c) **Resourceful,** that he may use to the best advantage whatever is at hand to prevent further damage, and to assist Nature's efforts to repair the mischief already done

d) **Dextrous,** that he may handle a patient without causing unnecessary pain, and use appliances efficiently and neatly.

e) **Explicit,** that he may give clear instructions to the patient or the bystanders how best to assist him.

f) **Discriminating,** that he may decide which of several injuries should be treated first.

g) **Persevering,** that he may continue his efforts, though not at first successful.

h) **Sympathetic,** that he may give real comfort and encouragement to the suffering.

the railway station. Joe Underwood, a musician in my maternal grandfather's band, also left them an inheritance. Bletchley had an active St John group for many years because of accidents at the railway station where First Aid was very important.

The Nursing Division operated a medical loans section from the shed at the back of the clinic. This was badly needed as there was no local hospital. These ladies were so devoted to voluntary work and were led by Miss Scobie and included Miss Taylor (Mum's hairdresser), Mrs Tebbit and Mrs Mead. One concert we performed was held in St Martin's Hall, when I was 10, and a photograph of it recently appeared on Facebook. One year I was part of a Morris Dancing group, with bells and ribbons on our ankles and using sticks to tap. Another year Mrs Walpole persuaded me to sing 'Loves old sweet song' in an old-time concert.

The enrolment ceremony was held in the Methodist Hall next to the Council Offices. About eight of us made our promises and recited the Cadet Code of Chivalry and we could then have a proper grey dress and black beret.

My enrolment into Cadets by Monica White

Miss Monica White, the County Staff Officer for Cadets, travelled from Marlow to conduct the enrolment ceremony and gave an encouraging talk. Study now began in earnest. We passed our Preliminary First Aid, then our Home Nursing exams, then proceeded to do the Child Care course and the Hygiene course. My ambition was to gain the Grand Prior's Badge. This was on a par with the Queen's Guide Award. We needed to pass twelve proficiency subjects and could only take up to four per year, so it would take at least three years plus regular attendance at meetings. Also, one was required to pass the annual First Aid re-exam and gain some voluntary hours partaking in public duties. Child care and hygiene counted, so did map reading, casualty make-up and games, which could be taken at the county camp. But that still left around six to achieve. My cycling proficiency counted, but my piano playing did not because there was a separate musician's badge.

I enlisted my domestic science teacher to help me gain the cookery badge and also the homecraft badge. Homecraft consisted of learning how to clean shoes and silver, how to spring clean cupboards, how to sew buttons on and how to hem trousers. We also learned how to set a table correctly and iron shirts and dresses.

I spent a day at the vet's one summer holiday and wrote a project on how to care for different animals. For International Friendship I had a pen pal in Brittany and regularly wrote to her, exchanging letters and cards. Another subject was Citizenship, where I learned about the Council, Government and civic life.

My friend at Cadets was Ann Crawford, who had five sisters, and I think most of them joined Cadets as they came of age. St John was a disciplined organisation and we had regular uniform inspections and learned basic drill. Every year an inspection would be held either just with the division or with the groups in the area or county. The first inspection that I

Bletchley's first Grand Prior's Cadet, 1965

attended was in 1958 when we went to Wolverton. One of the biggest ones for Buckinghamshire was the large county inspection in 1965 when Princess Margaret inspected us, travelling around the ranks in a Land Rover. I was chosen to carry the Cadet Flag, but it poured with rain and the water dripped off the flag on to my uniform.

Every year a County Camp was held at the end of July. The first one I attended was at Gower in South Wales. I enjoyed travelling there in a train that had compartments, but did not enjoy the week as I got very homesick. After this the camp was held for many years at Totland Bay, Isle of Wight. We would pretend that we were going abroad on the ferry to go over to the island. At first, we would send our luggage in advance and be required to take the kit bags to High Wycombe railway station. We would travel to Waterloo and on to Lymington by train. Double decker buses would be hired for the week on the island to transport us around.

Bucks County Cadet Camp, Totland Bay, Isle of Wight

Each morning one of the adults would walk around the girls' and boys' fields banging a saucepan and shouting, "It's time to get up, the sun's scorching your eyes, rise and shine everybody!" After breakfast at 8.00 am in the cadet mess, we had a 15-minute assembly and prayers. Then we went to study a proficiency subject. After a hearty cooked lunch, we would have free time to write postcards, or read, then we would line up by the flag pole and walk to one of the nearby beaches. We had our own lifeguards and there would be a sandcastle competition, or we would look for shells and seaweed and play games. After we arrived back at camp it was time to prepare for the evening's entertainment.

There would be a talent show on one evening and a concert performed by the adults another evening. Two evenings during the week a hall was booked to hold a disco and party. Some afternoons a trip was arranged to visit Robin's Hill, Godshill or Newport. Sometimes we would have a fire practice. When Richard Smith, the Town Crier for Beaconsfield, shouted "Fire", you really heard him and moved!

Our aim at camp was to win the tent shield competition. The shields would be displayed outside each tent from different groups around Bucks. We would also hope to win prizes for our part in the talent contest or the sandcastle competition. Some of the young adults would love to play tricks. The flag would often disappear and turn up in the duty officer's bedding etc, or there would be weird ghostly noises around a tent in the evenings.

Arthur Kingsbury, a County Staff Officer, filmed many of the camps and county reviews over the years and they would be shown to members at county events. They provide a permanent record of the leadership training given to young people and the best way to encourage First Aid and associated skills outdoors. Many friendships that were forged over the years around the county, continue to this day. The films have been put onto DVD and provide a lasting memory of comradeship and volunteering.

Another opportunity for training with other members from around the county was the adventure training weekend held at Green Park Youth Centre. It was often held in the spring and we would take part in exercises based around the grounds. This could be First Aid, rescue work or various incidents. It was a typical 1960s building, but lent itself to competitions and journeys to the nearby Wendover Woods. Each person had their own bedroom and the meals were excellent. Progressing from being one of the Cadets, I was asked later on to help run the groups and think up basic care work, health and safety scenarios or moving and handling sessions. The grounds and barn buildings were ideal for teenagers to have adventures and pursue rescue work. One year we learned about small planes and ejector seats from staff at nearby RAF Halton.

Green Park Adventure Weekend with Nancy Sale, 1969

In the autumn the nursing members could go to Missenden Abbey for a nursing weekend. Many of the St John nurses would choose a topic and develop it over the weekend. One year new disposable equipment was demonstrated and used. Some years there would be a guest speaker, and on one occasion Rosemary Bailey, the author of many nursing manuals, gave a talk. Another year Sir Harry Verney, a great nephew of Florence Nightingale, gave us a talk about her work at Claydon House. Sometimes I would be asked to play the piano for the short service. The hymn 'Praise my soul the King of heaven' was often used at St John events. On the Saturday evening we would entertain each other with songs, sketches or musical items. Wigs and dressing up were the order of the day.

One of the duties that we really looked forward to was the cloakroom duty at Wilton Hall. Every year the local Operatic Society would stage one of the lovely musicals of the 1950s, the Rodgers and Hammerstein era. The first one I saw was 'Rosemarie', and I was singing that song to my sister for weeks afterwards. I also saw 'South Pacific' (my favourite), 'Showboat', 'My Fair Lady' and 'Kismet', which I thoroughly enjoyed. Once we had collected all the coats on to the hooks in the cloakroom and given out the tickets, we were allowed to sit on the steps of the balcony to watch. There were never any spare seats as it always was a sell-out. Mr Gibbs, a tall handsome man with a fine voice, would take one of the leading parts and Mr Kay our school caretaker would be part of the chorus. Often Mrs Gibbs, the drama teacher, produced the show, Ray Holdom conducted the orchestra and Ron Waite was the first violinist. Ray Guntrip, a local caterer, was in charge of the refreshments.

Mrs Walpole, our officer, arranged with the Matron of a local County Council residential home, for the Cadets to undertake duties there at weekends. This was for two girls from 9.00 am until 1.00 pm. We would put our names on a rota when we could attend. After we had completed 200 hours, we would gain

Going on duty to The Coppice Care Home

our voluntary service badge to sew on the uniform. Mrs Shadlock, the Matron, became our Divisional President and gave us much encouragement to go into nursing. About a dozen girls eventually went to several hospitals for a nursing career.

Our duties would be to help hang the washing out or fetch it in, go into the bedrooms and wipe the washbasins and polish the taps. This would be when the residents were finishing their breakfast. Another job would be to roll up cotton wool balls for swabs. Later we would help serve the mid-morning drinks, arrange any flowers and chat to the residents. Some Sundays we would often help different residents go to the nearby St Mary's Church for the morning service. After our break we would set the tables for lunch and read the paper to the residents if they requested help. At 1.00 pm we could have some lunch with the staff, once the tables had been cleared and cleaned. Then they would sign our duty book and we would walk back home about a mile and a half.

When the family moved to Woburn Sands, Mum drove me to the meetings and when I went into the Nursing Division to take my adult First Aid and Home Nursing exams, Mum stayed and joined. Our adult certificates were presented by Dorian Williams, a famous sports presenter who lived locally and who was grateful for St John duties at the Whaddon Point-to-Points. On moving to Stoke Mandeville I joined the Aylesbury Nursing Division run by Miss Mabel Evans. Her sister, Amy, ran the Aylesbury Cadets and was the same strict Miss Evans from the hospital sewing room. I caught the hospital transport to Co-op corner, which was just opposite the headquarters, and Mrs Eaton, a member, would drive me back to Stoke Mandeville Hospital as she lived opposite. Her husband was headmaster of the Henry Floyd Grammar School. However, it was short lived attending Aylesbury, as the following year I took part in a First Aid Quiz held at the Wendover HQ and was invited to take charge of the Nursing Cadet Division there.

Presentation of Adult First Aid and Home
Nursing Certificates by Dorian Williams

It was at Wendover that I met my friend Kit Harrop. She had joined St John during the war when people were expected to do other duties after work, such as fire watching, or Air Raid Precaution (ARP) work. Kit decided to join St John after finishing her work at the ammunition factory down Bicester Road in Aylesbury. She used to tell stories of her shifts with the ambulance men, covering the evenings when the regular ambulance personnel were off duty. This was of course before the NHS and other places were often manned by St John. Kit had been ill and could not cope with running the Wendover Nursing Cadets anymore, so I took it on with her for guidance and support. Kit helped with a lot of the uniforms and the sewing of badges. She also helped when we took the Cadets on trips or to inspections, as well as with artwork for charts and shields. This was the start of a friendship that lasted for many years when Auntie Kit would babysit for my two young sons or make pies, do ironing, or contact people. She did anything to support me so that I was able to organise and run the division.

On duty at Wendover Fete, 1971

In 1968 my friend Dorothy was starting her enrolled nurse training. She had been in Bletchley Division with me, so she agreed to come and help me run the Nursing Cadets. It was separate groups at that time with the boys' division run by Bill Wright, assisted by Bob Nugent, who went on to become an ambulanceman. We were very proud of our girls and over the three years managed to help five of them gain the Grand Prior's Badge. The parents committee helped with fundraising at bazaars and rummage sales and we were one of the first divisions in Bucks to kit the girls out in the new grey nursing dress. Another highlight was a National Inspection in Hyde Park, London, by HRH Princess Anne, who had taken over as Commandant in Chief of Cadets from HRH Princess Margaret.

Another thrill was when Dorothy and I attended a leadership weekend at The Randolph Hotel, Oxford – some money was left from the King George VI fund for leadership training. We thoroughly enjoyed our sessions at the hotel, whilst meeting other keen young members from around the region. Some friends remained in touch for many years and were good contacts. We met the chaps from High Wycombe Division at socials; indeed, it was Bob Grace who gave a disco and party for Dot and myself in the Nurses' Home to celebrate our 21st birthdays.

Another tale with Dorothy was when we were at Kit and her aunt's house one Christmas Eve. We had been at the hospital carol singing around the wards and were staying at the house for a while until it was time to go to St Mary's Church, Wendover, for the Midnight Mass. Christmas Eve was Auntie Clark's birthday and her friend Mrs Hempstock had come over on the bus to celebrate it with her. Unfortunately, both ladies had partaken of too much sherry and the living room had become hot and stuffy, so much so that Mrs Hempstock suddenly keeled over. Dot and I treated her for a faint and wondered if she had suffered a TIA (transient ischaemic attack) so we telephoned for a GP to check her over. In a very short time, the doctor came tearing around just as Mrs Hempstock recovered and asked him if he would like a drink for Christmas!

Dorothy and I decided to have a Grand Presentation Evening in the Nurses' Gymnasium at Stoke Mandeville. We had five girls who were to be presented with their Grand Prior's Awards and I had written a pageant on the History of St John that the Cadets were to perform. One of the tutors would play the piano for us. We hired some costumes, persuaded a local florist to put a display of plants around the stage and borrowed some equipment from National Headquarters. My father, who was an auxiliary member at Bletchley, wanted to present the County HQ with a couch and we had lots of certificates and cups to present. We organised refreshments with the parents committee. All went well, but most of the area and county staff turned up to attend – apparently, I wasn't supposed to invite everyone, as they were supposed to take it in turn to visit different divisions! It turned out to be a long evening, but one that was remembered

Wendover Grand Prior Cadets at Presentation Evening, 1972

for many years. The Bucks Herald gave a good write up and we became one of the best nursing cadet groups in Bucks at that time.

After working as a Staff Nurse for six months on the Men's Surgical Ward, I was shortly to move to Northampton to study Midwifery, so I handed over the division to my sister, who was by then undergoing her nurse training at Stoke Mandeville. Heidi Mason, a nurse from Wendover, also ran it with Rosemary.

CHAPTER 12
A LIFE OF CARING

My first interview for a job in the community went well. The only problem was that the vacancy was for the Buckingham area and I lived in Aylesbury, 18 miles away. The senior nurses said that they thought I was suitable for the job, but that I would need to wait for a vacancy in Aylesbury. This vacancy occurred in February 1979 and I started on 19th March as a Community Psychiatric Nurse for the elderly. My patch was to include the villages of Haddenham, Long Crendon, Brill, Waddesdon and Whitchurch, a large rural area on the borders of Oxfordshire. Carol George had the villages to the south of Aylesbury, including Princes Risborough and Wendover and Radha Corina was overseeing Aylesbury town itself. At the start, my hours were a forty-hour week and to be home based. This was important as the job paid for a land line telephone and petrol expenses.

The salary was £3,489-£4,464 with £130 flat rate supplement. I started with only eight patients on my caseload and a three-week induction to the surgeries and area. North Bucks and the Aylesbury area were combined before Milton Keynes became established. We would have joint meetings at Tindal Hospital with their community staff on a Tuesday, then go to The Red Lion in Bierton for lunch. It was a very pleasant easy-going job in those days.

I attended meetings at the health centres and surgeries and the caseload gradually rose to 35 clients. I became friendly with our department's young social worker, Gill Rowe. She wanted to attend a course on the Care of the Elderly in Oxford spread over six Fridays and my nursing officer, Mr Pat Beale, agreed that it would be beneficial for my ongoing learning to also go on the course. Dr Muir Gray, a specialist consultant for the elderly, was one of our lecturers and is now a senior Government spokesman on elderly policies. That was the first specialised training for the job that I received. Many other courses would follow, such as the ENB 940 Care of the Elderly Course and the Community Diploma Course, held at Northampton.

At the time providing a community service to the elderly mentally ill was a new concept. Traditionally the psycho geriatrics (as they were called then) were nursed in huge wards in psychiatric or geriatric hospitals. The consultant at the time, Dr White, had far reaching ideas during the 1970s and persuaded the health authorities to close most of the wards and trial a community service; our ward would be the 35 patients in each CPN's area. We received many visitors to witness this service and I remember a group from the National Volunteer Bureau from Berkhamsted and a senior nurse coming to observe from Swansea. One day I took the Bucks County Medical Officer of Health out on my visits to show him my caseload.

Every day was different. Sometimes we would be asked for help for difficult clients in County Council homes, or other times we might be asked to give training sessions to student nurses or home helps. I got to know many of the local people in that area and became friends with the district nurses and health visitors.

When I started, Dr Gaminiratne was senior registrar for the department, and when Dr Gore retired, 'Dr Gamini' became my new boss. I ended up working with him for 26 years. He retired in May 2005 and I followed in June that same year. The numbers of troubled clients within the community were much fewer in those days, and we were so familiar with many of the regulars that it became almost a revolving door for some of the clients.

Dr Roy Simons, the consultant for High Wycombe, thought that the Community Psychiatric Nurses could be very proactive in providing early mental health care in the community. He encouraged the nurses to set up day clubs in several locations. His idea was to help the 'grey area', who were early problem people to try to stop them developing into full-blown health problems. Loneliness, isolation, poverty and loss could all be addressed at a very early stage.

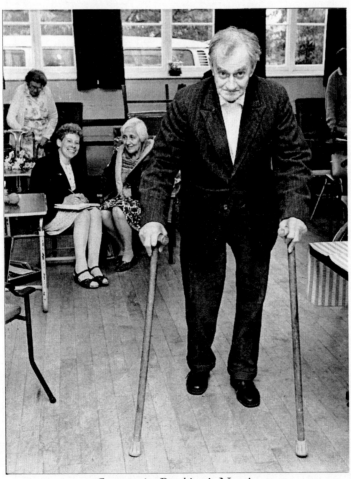

Community Psychiatric Nursing

There were many elderly people in Haddenham which was a large village on my patch. Many local people wanted to volunteer to support community projects so it seemed an ideal place to start a day club, and I had my experience from St John Ambulance of working with volunteers to rally support. This was to be called the Thursday Club to remind clients when it was held. Initially I set it up with Gill Rowe and a dozen people in the lounge of some council sheltered flatlets. Unfortunately, one gentleman lost his way to the toilet, urinated outside a flat and the resident complained. I had learned an important lesson from this situation, which I used to develop my Thursday Club into a valuable community asset – I held the club in a neutral venue or hall, with not too many exits! I started the club with, approximately, six clients and worked the numbers upwards gradually, at the same time increasing the volunteer's ratio to the number of clients, so that there was always plenty of supervision.

I applied for grants from Social Services and local charities. We met in the smaller room of the village hall at first, and Sue Peck, a trained physiotherapist, volunteered her help and the community supported us and came forward to volunteer. We provided ongoing training and affiliated ourselves to Bucks Association for Mental Health.

Our first outing/trip was to visit the shops at Central Milton Keynes. Many of the relatives had not had the opportunity to visit the new centre and we had a lunch in the Woolworths cafeteria. It was all on the flat and ideal for the elderly. Eventually councillors petitioned for a purpose-built day centre in Haddenham and it was a grand day when I was invited by the County Council to attend the opening ceremony. It would be run by The Buckinghamshire Red Cross, as they already ran other day centres in Bucks.

The next day club was to be in Waddesdon in September 1981. Waddesdon had many elderly people who had worked on the

Health Education sessions at Waddesdon Club

Waddesdon Manor Estate and lived mainly in two streets, Quainton Road and Frederick Street. Mary Norris, caretaker of the little Catholic Hall in Frederick Street, was keen to help a club get started as it would bring in some revenue for the hall, but the only problem was that meals could not be cooked there. Over the years, meals came from Manor House Hospital, The WRVS Meals on Wheels and Grendon Underwood Prison. This would be called the Wednesday Club, as, if needed, clients could have two days care, providing we could find voluntary drivers to ferry them back and forth. We had many loyal drivers over the years who were paid petrol expenses and proved reliable supporters.

Two outstanding volunteers emerged to keep the Waddesdon Club going each and every week. Pat Wright was very active in the village and became devoted in a support role and Audrey Pegg was a local home help. Her family were growing up and she worked closely with Pat to ensure that the room was ready, heating on, chairs and tables cleaned and all ready to commence each Wednesday. The local clergy came to provide Services and another lady would give exercise classes.

Over the years the parish councils gave small grants, Waddesdon Manor Charitable Trust helped and Westcott Social Club raised money for outings. I became quite good over the years in obtaining referrals from social services, district nurses, relatives and the day hospital to keep the numbers up. Other clubs followed, mainly Quainton Day Club in 1984 and St John Men's Club when I was moved later in my career to oversee the Aylesbury area.

The clubs were organised so that they worked in conjunction with other community services. If Meals on Wheels was Mondays and Wednesday in a village, the day club would be on a Tuesday or Thursday. If home care was more available certain

Long Crendon Day Club's 10th Birthday Party

days I would try and run a club on a different day to supplement services. This was important when Long Crendon day club started. Many relatives wanted to go into Thame for the market on Tuesdays, so the club was held Tuesdays to enable the relatives to have a break and go shopping. The Village Centre was ideal for this club as it was the right size. Many of the clients were familiar with the building as many years ago it had been their school. Delia Cave became their first organiser, supported by Pat Reid and Nora Ing.

One day as I was coming out of Haddenham Day Centre, I was chatting to Phyl Saw who visited elderly groups to provide exercises for the elderly and had been very active with Age Concern in Haddenham. Delia Cave retired as she was looking after her invalid husband and Phyl took up the post as organiser at Long Crendon. This was the start of many active years of day care, with the club eventually meeting on Tuesdays and Thursdays with a waiting list. Clients came from Brill, Worminghall, Oakley, Cuddington and Chearsley. Some drivers would bring two lots of clients to the club, which was a big help. These were the golden days of voluntary care in the community.

We also had many more options for care. The Cromwell Ward at Stoke Mandeville provided respite care for clients with organic illness i.e. advancing dementia, and Harding Ward provided admission for patients with functional illnesses, mainly depression, anxiety states or bipolar illness. The building had been part of the young disabled unit and was ideal, as it was on the flat and had wide doors for easy mobility. The thought at the time was that if a patient became physically ill, they were on the general hospital site to obtain an X-ray or blood test etc, to access services. This was a great improvement from the old facilities at Tindal Hospital, and community staff had offices opposite the wards which enabled good communication and liaison. Our unit was officially opened in 1991 by Rt Hon Virginia Bottomley, Minister for Health, who spent time

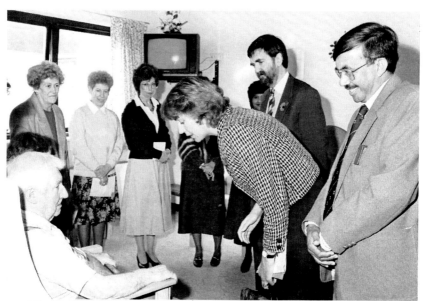

The Rt Hon Virginia Bottomley visits the John Hampden Unit, 1992

The John Hampden Unit
Aylesbury Vale Healthcare

CARE AT HOME
COMMUNITY MENTAL HEALTH TEAMS

speaking to the staff and patients and the CPNs. By this time, we also had Community Health Care Assistants who were introduced to her.

The main role of the Community Psychiatric Nurse was to support patients and their relatives in the community. Many of the patients needed our support as they had behavioural problems and were difficult to care for. We would need to assess them on referrals from GPs or our consultant and could then plan their care. This might be to refer to Social Services for a social worker or home help. They might require an assessment at our day hospital and specialised hospital day care or they might require an admission. We could discuss the cases at team meetings and would be able to obtain respite care for the people with dementia, if required. We could also check that the family had applied for the attendance allowance and refer them to Citizens Advice for help or housing services if applicable. Some needed to move to sheltered flats and others might require our health care assistants for support. Another role was to visit the chronic patients in group houses and administer the long-acting depot injections, which enabled those with a chronic mental health condition to remain stable.

Every year we would be given a student mental health nurse to teach and supervise, whilst they gained vital community experience. Some students would find this work easier than others and they needed to be able to plan their work and organise their time. The placement would involve learning and practising giving the oily depot injections and calling in at a variety of homes. They spent time at a day club to learn how they ran, devise funding ideas and observe how they were organised. They also spent time assisting and observing the work of the community mental health nursing assistants and how to liaise with other services. Towards the end of the placement they were given a small caseload to follow.

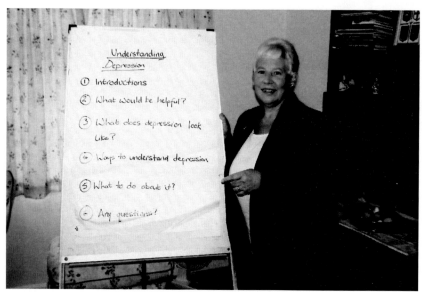

Teaching Sessions to Nursing Homes

Many hours were spent visiting people in their own homes. One day I could be going into a mansion with many rooms and a swimming pool and another I could be in a filthy cottage with insects crawling around, but I loved the variety it brought me in my daily routine.

When I started, some of the GP surgeries were held at the side of their houses, or in small office type rooms, but over the years much better purpose-built surgeries came into operation. I was invited to the opening of both the Waddesdon Surgery, and Haddenham Surgery which was moved to much larger premises on the edge of the village, with the pharmacy next-door. The Long Crendon Surgery was in the Old Chapel and had been adapted for a much different use. Brill Surgery was in the village square, with the pharmacy included, and I would also visit Thame Health Centre which had two groups of practices in the large health centre. I had to ensure that I went to the GPs who covered Buckinghamshire, not Oxfordshire, as it was on the border. In those days we had Thame Cottage Hospital for admissions and some respite, and Buckingham Hospital, which could provide beds so that the acute beds at Stoke Mandeville could be freed up.

During the 1980s and '90s, we had a very good relationship with the Council Home Help Service. A specialist home help organiser would attend our meetings and we often undertook joint visits with them to make a care plan. It worked well as a comprehensive service for the elderly mentally ill. Gradually with reorganisations and new ideas the services were cut. Agencies would provide home care and respite admissions would be undertaken in private care homes, paid from a different benefit system. Sometimes our job would be to act as an advocate to speak up for someone who was not able to speak up for themselves; other times it might be to push for better conditions with housing groups.

The Department of Mental Health for the Elderly, as it was later called, was very supportive of on-going training. After completing the teaching and assessing ENB 998 in October 1995, I went on to complete the City and Guilds Training and Skills Assessor course in January 1997. Each area had two Health Care Assistants (HCA) and they were encouraged to undertake the National Vocational Training to further their work and career. This did help two of the younger staff to progress their nursing careers. One undertook midwifery training, the other became a Registered General Nurse. One HCA that I mentored, did a terrific amount of studying to gain her Level 3 NVQ award, but a new charge nurse on her ward did not encourage her or give her any credit for the experience and so she left to get a better job in a nursing home. I felt that it was our loss for the unit. After the millennium, this service was gradually cut. As Health Care Assistants left, they were not replaced.

My favourite ward was Harding Ward where people were suffering from depression and they took time to improve, but the results were impressive. With a combination of occupational therapy, antidepressants and talking therapies, many were able to go home and resume their lives. That proved so rewarding that I liked to work some night shifts there and help the patients to get a good night's sleep. Often, they would like to talk over their worries in the night and on discharge would have day care booked to attend the day hospital.

John, my husband, was made redundant at the age of 50, but was able to obtain a job on Cromwell Ward. Dave Moore, the manager, was always looking for patient, caring, gentle staff – not many people wanted to work with elderly people suffering from dementia. John had passed his home nursing exams with St John and had taken part in the care competitions, so he gave it a go! This worked very well for six months, but he managed to find an electrical and maintenance job with regular hours at RAF Halton, and enjoyed working there until he retired at 65.

Occasionally a drug representatives' lunch would be organised, when they would bring a buffet lunch into the seminar room and speak to the staff about new medication or treatments. We listened carefully, but often took the information 'with a pinch of salt' as they were obviously paid to promote their product. Sometimes they would bring along notepads, pens and samples to distribute, which livened up proceedings and helped with team building. When it became the fashion for team building days, we went to a hotel in Buckingham one year and the Weston Turville Golf Club another year.

I completed the Diploma of Higher Education in 1995 with the Certificate in Community Nursing. This enabled me to update and increase my knowledge and kept my job secure for the future. The course was for a year at Nene College, Northampton, now a university. We were required to produce five assignments and go on three placements to gain more psychiatric experience. My lifeline was a nursing friend, called Arlett, who lived at Buckingham. We shared lifts together and helped each other study. The larger group consisted of school

Diploma in Community Nursing, 1995

nurses, district nurses and our eight community psychiatric nurses. One day a week we would attend our own speciality and another day was for study. At the end of the course we undertook a three-hour community mental health examination. For my three placements, I first arranged to work with the under-65 mental health team based at Tindal Hospital. The second placement was with another nurse from an elderly mental health team and the third placement was at the Milton Keynes Elderly Day Hospital near Wolverton. Our three most interesting visits during the year were to a secure unit at Birmingham, Broadmoor High Security Hospital and The London Lighthouse Unit for patients suffering from HIV/Aids.

On my return the department was now called the John Hampden Unit for the Elderly Mentally Ill. I moved to the Aylesbury town area as I had worked in the villages for 16 years. Town work was different as, although there were more facilities, there was not as much support from the community volunteers or neighbours. The number of referrals was much greater, the work was changing, and team meetings each week gave out the referrals to the most suitable clinician. GPs now referred to the team, not to individual CPNs.

In 1998 the National Health Service was fifty years old and there were many programmes about its formation. Health Service staff were invited to bid for a ticket to attend the celebration service to be held in Westminster Abbey on 3rd July 1998, and I put my name forward and was selected to attend. As we queued up to enter the Abbey I recognised a few staff from Aylesbury, including Roger Titley, but the special guests that I remember were Simon Hughes MP and Betty Boothroyd, who was Speaker of the House of Commons.

After the service everyone walked over the road to the Queen Elizabeth Hall where a buffet lunch was provided. Staff were then free to spend the day as they liked in London. I walked along to Westminster Pier and had a lovely afternoon on a

Community Psychiatric Nurse 1979-2005

pleasure boat ride, having all the famous sights of London pointed out to me.

Back on duty in Aylesbury, I was asked to assess and help a man with mental health problems and I realised that I had nursed his mother previously. In another village I had a daughter referred who was 65, and I still had her mother on my caseload, who was 95! I had been in this role for 26 years and it would soon be time to step down. This came on 17th June 2005. I had enough years in the Health Service for my pension and it was time for some more adventures.

The John Hampden Unit gave me a good send off. A buffet lunch was held in the seminar room and I was presented with flowers and vouchers. Sandy Barnes wrote a poem about me called 'Valerie the Whirlwind', which gave everyone a laugh and was so very true. Aylesbury Social Services were represented and gave me a card and a dozen red roses, and they said that I had saved Social Services a lot of money with the day clubs. Several relatives, student nurses, care assistants and patients sent their best wishes and the clubs presented me with more vouchers. I had worked in the National Health Service for thirty-eight years, but now it was time for the next chapter in my life!

My leaving presentation, 17th June, 2005

VALERIE: THE WHIRLWIND

You see the dust then the whirl,
Until finally Val sits at her desk with a final twirl.
But do not blink, as she'll be gone
Off on a home visit or to the day centre to lead a quiz or a singsong.

Now voluntary day centres is an area that Val does best;
She started developing them in 1979 with great zest.
From Haddenham and Waddesdon, to Quainton and Long Crendon,
She worked with many a generation.

Val liaised with doctors and nurses and carers throughout the countryside,
Until she moved patches, but the day care didn't slide.
As moving from rural areas to the Aylesbury Team,
Val thought something was lacking for the men who didn't fit into the mainstream.
So a plan she did hatch for this Aylesbury patch,
With the idea of the Men's Club at St John's ; this for the men was a perfect match.

Val's been a general and mental health nurse;
To her, the patients have always come first.
She worked on surgical wards and worked nights,
In her smart nurse's uniform and brown tights.
But the community and St John Ambulance is where her heart does belong,
Attending pop and classical concerts, parades and garden fetes, Val will be in the throng.

Val has been part of various carers groups for many a year,
With Relatives Support and the Sitting Service, she has shown enthusiasm and no fear.
Even if there has been red tape and budgets with money to find,
Val has been campaigning with mental health in mind.

Val has travelled to Rome, Pakistan, Zimbabwe, all to lend them her skills;
Teaching first aid so the people there can care for all ills.
But Val is now retiring and we wish you well in all the places you go and all that you do,
Though just remember your friends here will want to hear all about it too.

And one last thing, Jerusalem had better watch out,
Because Val, this whirlwind, is soon to be about.

Love, Sandie

CHAPTER 13
STORIES FROM MY CPN CASELOAD

I liked being out and around in the community, but it could be cold in winter and hot in the car during the summer. Once I took a senior nursing officer on visits, as he wanted to observe the work. It was one of the hottest days of the year and he took his jacket off in my car, but insisted on wearing it in the houses. He had a shirt and tie on also and he was taking his jacket on and off all day. Fortunately, I just had a comfortable dress on. I kept a thick coat and other clothes to wear, as well as some reserves, in the boot of my car for the worst of the weather in winter.

One day I was asked to visit an elderly lady in the village of Wing as the GP wanted me to assess her mental state. I knocked on the door and she let me in to have a chat. She seemed very well and capable, but as the conversation progressed she suddenly said, "I think you should be visiting my cousin next-door as she has memory problems." The surgery had given me the wrong house number and the two spinster cousins lived next-door to each other.

Once I had three ladies who had mental health problems and they lived next to each other in a row of old terraced houses. One had a husband, but this couple proved to be very difficult and would not accept help. Next-door lived a timid lady who was very vulnerable and I managed to arrange some effective community support for her. The third lady suffered from depression and she had had a psychotic episode during the war and shot her son during an argument. After several years in Broadmoor Hospital, she came to live near her brother, but the stress and guilt over the years had caused chronic depression. She was helped with a place at the day club and community support visits.

One Christmas I visited a lady who suffered from schizophrenia and she chased me along the garden path with a yard brush! She had been withdrawn and been chair bound for several days and I was trying to persuade her to come to hospital for help. She suddenly started screaming threats at me and got up to chase me. I managed to run down the path and go in my car back to the hospital. Later in the day she was sectioned and therefore forced to come into hospital for treatment.

Another psychotic patient who required sectioning was blaspheming by the altar of St Mary's Church, Aylesbury. When he became well, after admission, he was the most pleasant and friendly of gentlemen.

Another lady became ill after her husband died and could be found lying on his grave at the cemetery. She could not be persuaded to have the depot injections, so was sectioned for a spell in hospital. After that I visited her to give the injection every three weeks for many years. Dr Gamini was very keen that we befriend the patients, as the elderly are often isolated and have no one to talk to or discuss matters. If the nurse could build a good rapport with the person they could be helped and supported at home for much longer, rather than having to go into a home.

One referral had asked me to visit a huge man twice my size, who had personality problems and he needed to be assessed. The doctor wanted me to visit alone, but I resisted, as my gut feeling was that I needed a male nurse to accompany me as the man disliked women and could be aggressive. A male CPN and myself visited and he was able to encourage the man to accept help. We stayed by the door for a quick exit, but he mellowed on seeing the male nurse.

During one summer, I visited a lady to give her the depot injection. She fancied herself as a clairvoyant and wanted to read the tea leaves in my tea cup and she also read my palm. The only prophecy I can remember is that she said that I would live near a river. As I was well established in Aylesbury that did not seem very likely. Now years on I live at Christchurch, where two rivers, the Stour and the Avon, run into the sea!

Sometimes I was fed and watered well. I was asked to visit my ex-science teacher who was now running a pub. The GP wanted me to assess his mother. When I arrived, he and his wife were just having a late breakfast, so he said, "Come and join us." Another time I was visiting a retired doctor who was in the middle of his garden enjoying a garden party. The garden was huge with a swimming pool and I was invited to partake of the strawberry tea!

Hoarding is often a problem with the elderly as the souvenirs give them so many happy memories. I visited one gentleman who had old papers and magazines piling up to the ceiling everywhere in his house. One could only squeeze along a narrow corridor to go into any room. He came in for an admission as he was neglecting himself and eventually had to surrender to full-time care. One of the council residential homes had an upstairs corridor in the building where several men lived, as they had been on their own and could not cope in the community. They might have chronic depression or even early dementia at only 60 years of age.

One day I did a joint visit with the psychologist to a difficult gentleman who was an alcoholic. The flat was filthy and the council said that it was a health risk to other people in the flats. The psychologist could see that the man would not be suitable for any therapy and he went in the residential home and did quite well with a care plan and the comradeship of the other men. Another patient was a lady who kept collecting toiletries and a lot of clothes and ornaments from charity shops. She came

157

into the ward to enable the relatives to clear the flat, which was fine for a time but after a few months the flat would be just as bad. Another time, I was given two sisters to visit in a housing association flat. These two petite sisters were like little mice. They shared a meal on wheels lunch and would not spend much money. I managed to persuade them to spend two days each week at my clubs, where they ate a jolly good meal. Unfortunately, they put rubbish, cooking oil and old food down the pipes in the flat and caused a blockage along the whole building, which did not help their cause to stay at home!

Another lady flooded the place. She left the kitchen taps running and went to sit in the lounge to watch the television. The worst part was when she realised the kitchen floor was flooded – she stood in the kitchen water with a two-bar electric fire to dry it out. Her relatives were most indignant when we said she needed care. She was already eating old food and wandering the village in the evenings, because she was lonely. It became too risky for my Health Care Assistants to visit her with the old electrics and flooding.

I even had a gentleman referred who lived in a caravan. He had dementia and his wife was trying valiantly to care for him. They were ex-fair workers living in a cluster of caravans together and he was able to visit other retired workers in other caravans for a time. Eventually it all got too much and his wife had to let him go into care. A caravan is far too small to look after someone who is restless. One gentleman managed to leave the house one evening as he must have found some money, and went to the railway station as he thought that he was due at work. He managed to get as far as Birmingham before being apprehended by the Police.

One very interesting patient, who suffered from depression, told me that she was a descendant of Elizabeth Fry, the prison reformer, and she showed me some papers which I was amazed to read. We had many fascinating talks over time. Another lady had a paranoid illness and imagined that she could see children sitting on some of her chairs. She suffered from loneliness and I encouraged her to attend the day clubs. She would bring her silver cutlery in her large handbag, as she was frightened that the burglars would take her possessions whilst she had gone out.

A referral letter from a GP one day asked me to visit a lady in a village. The address was 'Well Cottage', but there was no street or house number. I drove around the village looking for a well, but that had long gone. The postman pointed me to the cottage and the well now had flowers covering the top. The lady was known in the area and quite a character. She had grown up in Belgium and spoke fluent Flemish. During the Second World War she had been a secret agent and had been parachuted behind enemy lines. The only problem was that she had landed on a cow! Luckily, she wasn't hurt and managed to make contact with her people.

Mrs A came to the day club and told many amusing stories. Unfortunately, her recent memory was very poor, she required increasing supervision over the months and needed much persuasion to give up driving, as she was a very independent lady.

Some of the villages were quite a way from Aylesbury and I remember one lady had about twenty cats in her bungalow and it was becoming a health hazard. The neighbours complained to the council, so gradually homes were found for most of the cats with the help of a local animal charity and the remaining ones neutered. Another lady from that village was excellent at sewing and making soft toys. She came to the Long Crendon Club and made many craft items for the sales. Mrs C made me a large Golly doll that I still treasure. I was very sorry when she couldn't cope on her own anymore and moved to a residential home.

One patient found my home telephone number in the BT phone book and started phoning me in the evenings. Her family doctor had a word with her and a neighbour called around to have a chat with her at tea time. This community care in the villages made the job so worthwhile. Many mental health problems were caused by loneliness and isolation and were helped by attending the day clubs where problems could be picked up early and sorted.

One family did not want me to visit early. They said, "Let the streets air, Val, before you do the rounds." As already mentioned, my nickname was Valerie the Whirlwind, as I liked to keep on top of my workload. I wanted to visit patients in the mornings and get back before the school pick-ups and rush hour traffic began, as it was a nightmare travelling along the Mandeville Road and finding a parking spot back at the hospital! I would avoid writing notes for half the day and preferred brief but regular visits to manage my caseload. Other nurses in the department took a different approach and ended up wasting valuable time stuck in traffic or bogged down in paperwork.

Another interesting aspect of the job was visiting various residential and nursing homes. Difficult patients whom the staff were not coping with would be referred for us to give advice on their management, or to assess if an admission to the unit would improve their condition. I visited one such gentleman in a council residential home who had already had an admission to our unit, but the staff were still having problems. He would refuse help and not allow the staff to care for him or feed him. He was going to require more specialist help at Chiltern View Nursing Home. I asked the doctors for help with some sedation so that the staff could help him until a bed became available. This was duly given, but sadly soon afterwards the patient passed away. A Coroner's Court was held in which I was asked to attend and give information. Luckily my notes and records were all up to date! The patient's relatives were upset that he had died and could not accept that he was suffering and deteriorating. Soon after that I was due to go on holiday and I was very glad to have that break!

My eldest patient was a 100-year-old lady, who suffered from paranoia and often had delusions of children sitting in her living room. My health care assistants would visit her and help with shopping and bathing, but she could be difficult. One day she would not answer the door and cried out that she was locked in the bungalow and could not see her keys. I went around the back of the bungalow and asked her to open the bedroom window and pass me a chair... so my climbing into the Nurses' Home came in very useful. (This was before Health and Safety!) I climbed in and found her keys. She settled down once the anxiety of the lost keys had passed and was happy to come with me to day care. On her 100th birthday, the care assistants and myself took her out for a meal as she was lonely and such a character.

Sometimes the relatives were more of a problem than the patient as they could not accept the care that was required and were often in denial. Many thought that the patient would improve. Sometimes, as with multi-infarct dementia (due to their poor circulation), they would have better days, but those suffering from Alzheimer's disease would progressively deteriorate. Education about dementia and Alzheimer's disease was sparse during my early CPN days but eventually carers groups, the Alzheimer's Society and charities provided education and training to support carers.

Bill Bartlett was the hospital group's treasurer. His wife developed early dementia when she was in her sixties and he nursed her at home for several years. We managed to support him by giving her five days day care. This enabled him to continue his work in the treasurer's office. After she had died, he decided to start a support group for relatives and carers struggling to cope with an elderly relative. This ran one evening a month for many years. I liked to attend the meetings as it let me witness another side of the community role. Bill worked with Roger Titley and agreed to become Treasurer of the Bedgrove St John Adult Division.

CHAPTER 14
WOULD YOU CARE TO JOIN ME?

Whilst in Northampton, Paul and I did try the men's division of the St John Ambulance at the County Headquarters, Billing Road, as there were still separate men and women's groups. I went along as a nurse and gave one or two care training sessions to the men's group. They had a bar in the social room and Paul's GP at the time, Dr Bantock, was one of the divisional surgeons, and he actually bought me a drink. One or two evenings I went along to the Cadet Division at Newport Pagnell, as it was very good to experience and observe other people's ways of running things.

In 1974, Paul and I made our home at Bedgrove, Aylesbury, and wanted to continue in St John, so we thought we would try Leighton Buzzard Adult Division. By this time it was a combined group with Peter Lymbery as their Superintendent. The members were a happy, friendly group and again I assisted them with some care evenings and helped them acquire some home nursing equipment. We undertook a variety of duties, from gymkhanas and horse trials, to the town's carnival, as Peter was a leading figure in the town and had many connections. This association and particularly our friendship with the officers, Angela and Phyllis, continued for many years.

We saw the need for a youth group on Bedgrove Estate and wanted to form a Cadet Division. To do this we had to persuade some St John Ambulance County Officers that we could run it and would not leave it as soon as we started a family. There was a precedent in the county as High Wycombe had Castlefield and

Booker Cadet Division, where the Cadets helped recruitment to Adult Divisions.

Miss Nancy Sale and Mr Bill Gibbs were the officers who grilled us at the County Headquarters. Would we be able to gain the parents' support? How would we raise funds? What training courses could we provide? How did we propose to do public duties? These and other questions had to be addressed. Bill Gibbs particularly liked our idea of washing cars and Nancy Sale was impressed with our view on planning incidents in Bedgrove Park and covering duties at the many local fetes.

Some trial meetings started in our lounge with some bandaging and First Aid sessions. We cut up old sheets to make triangular bandages and borrowed a Resusci-Anne model from County Headquarters. After discussions at The Church of the Holy Spirit, it was agreed that we could hold our meetings there on Monday evenings with a very cheap hire charge.

It was all a sharp learning curve. Arthur Pearce from Aylesbury Division came to examine the youngsters for the First Aid exam and failed the lot! He said they needed more practice and experience. Also, we required someone in the community with some influence to help us raise funds. Along came Roger Titley; he was the General Manager for the Aylesbury hospitals and his two daughters wanted to join the group. He agreed to become our President and was able to help us obtain grants from the Rotary Club and Harding Trust. Four other parents helped at the meetings, especially Bill Holliday, who was the pharmacist at St John's Hospital.

So started twelve happy years with Cadets. The children were bright and took part in the County Competitions. Sometimes we won the individual cups and other times the First Aid or Home Nursing Competitions. When we got through to the Regional Finals our main competitors were often Cadets from Dorset, which was part of the region. Many of those children made careers in the Health Service. Some became Senior Nurses,

Bedgrove Cadets with the Cup at the County AGM, 1978

one was a GP, another became an Anaesthetist and another a Health Visitor. One of the boys rose up the ranks in the Fire Service, two became Paramedics and another two girls became Occupational Therapists. One boy became a training officer for the British Heart Foundation and another became a St John trainer. A member emigrated to New Zealand and is manager of a large St John charity shop in the capital, Wellington. Our President, Mr Roger Titley, when he retired from the Heath Service, became our County St John Commander.

Each year we participated in the Adventure Training Weekend at Green Park Training Centre and every year we took a contingent of boys and girls to the County Cadet camp on the Isle of Wight. One year we held our own divisional camp at Green Park with our own First Aid tent and equipment borrowed from the Scouts.

Award Winners Bedgrove Cadets, 1980

Some memorable events occurred during those years. One was the St John Cadet Spectacular held at the Royal Albert Hall, London. This was on 9th October 1982 to celebrate the Diamond Jubilee of St John Cadets. Different counties were invited to enter for the event. On the day there would be a rehearsal in the morning and two performances in the afternoon and evening. Marks and Spencer were to sponsor all the refreshments and various professional well-known entertainers performed in between the cadet acts. Isla St Clair and Bill Pertwee were among them.

Buckinghamshire decided to give a keep fit display and my job was to take one of our members (a keep fit instructor) around the divisions for rehearsals. The five-minute display was to the music of Match of the Day. Around 75 Cadets wearing different coloured tee-shirts gave a synchronised display, and on Bill Gibbs' insistence, I appeared at the introduction as the organiser. Other memorable acts were some handbell ringers, a cadet band

and community singing. HRH Princess Anne as Commandant in Chief of Cadets of was the senior Royal present at the evening display. The visit did give me a chance to have a good look around the back rooms of the auditorium and see the different levels of the building, as the refreshments were served on the top level.

Bucks Keep Fit Display at the Royal Albert Hall

HRH Princess Anne opening the stable block building, May 1982

I met HRH Princess Anne again when she opened the new stable block building at Green Park during 1982 and at a garden party in the grounds of Buckingham Palace in 1983. At Green Park we gave a display with the Resusci-Anne model and also one of bedmaking. She asked how long I had been in St John and about my nurse training.

The other special national event during those years was on 20th June 1987. A great St John Party was held in Hyde Park, London. This was to celebrate the centenary of the St John Ambulance Brigade. It was a beautiful day with sunshine and many happy faces. Five and a half thousand entertainers and exhibitors agreed to donate their services. There were many displays, amusements, pageants, mock battles and an arena of events. Balloons were released and face painting was the order of the day. HM The Queen (The Sovereign Head) and HRH

Prince Philip were in attendance, and also The Grand Prior, HRH Duke of Gloucester and HRH the Duchess of Gloucester. It was organised by Major Peter Parker who was well known for his managing of the Royal Tournaments. It included a funfair, mock seaside, African dancers, knights in armour, a Police horse display and JCBs dancing in the arena. What a day out!

Other special duties that I remember from those times were when I was on duty at Mentmore Towers near Leighton Buzzard when the contents of the house were being sold by Sotheby's and the Hon Angus Ogilvy was in attendance. HRH The Queen opened the Civic Offices and Library at Central Milton Keynes and I was on duty. This time I was placed at the corner of a street where the royal cars were parked, which enabled me to witness all the bouquets being stored in the vehicles, including many small gifts from the crowds.

When our family came along, Barbara Gardner, the parent of one of our star Cadets, would babysit for us on the Monday evenings. Barbara was a teacher at Halton and was excellent at amusing children. Later my friend Kit helped a lot, especially with sewing, ironing, posters and display boards. Many people helped the Cadets gain their proficiency subjects. For Child Care, I would bath my children when they were babies in front of the Cadets. For Homecraft, a visit to our house on a Saturday morning to undertake various tasks was the order of the day. One parent helped with the Care of Animals, and a staff officer came along to teach History of the Order. One year we managed to produce six Grand Prior Cadets and held a special presentation evening. The Cadets gained voluntary hours at Manor House Fete, Bedgrove Day in the Park, Shaftesbury House, The Chestnuts Elderly Care Home and Aylesbury Carnival.

CHAPTER 15
THE LARGER FAMILY

I was given a promotion in 1982 and became Area Staff Officer for Cadets. This involved visiting other divisions for support and assisting at county training events. It was in 1982 that I heard that I was to be appointed to the Order of St John as a Serving Sister for services to Buckinghamshire St John.

1983 proved to be a very special year as Stephen arrived in April of that year. There were then three special St John events. I attended the Investiture at St John's Gate Clerkenwell, accompanied by Kit. She had been ill when her Serving Sister Award was given, so she came to mine instead. I remember Sir Peter Parker, head of British Rail, was one of the other recipients that day. Paul and I were then given an invitation to represent Bucks St John at one of the summer gardens parties at Buckingham Palace. We queued up with the other guests and some people thought that we were on duty. They got a shock when we produced our invitations.

Lasting memories included enjoying the bands situated at each end of the garden, alternating playing the music. Another memory is the dainty tea with finger sandwiches and cakes served in large marquees. It was lovely to see so many ladies in beautiful hats and men in suits. Some Bishops were there in morning dress, and there were many uniformed people from other organisations. As this was before the Palace was open each summer to the public, it was marvellous to walk through the plush rooms to the gardens at the back. A walk around the gardens was also a privilege. The Cadet Spectacular at the Royal Albert Hall was the third special St John event.

Buckingham Palace Garden Party, 1982

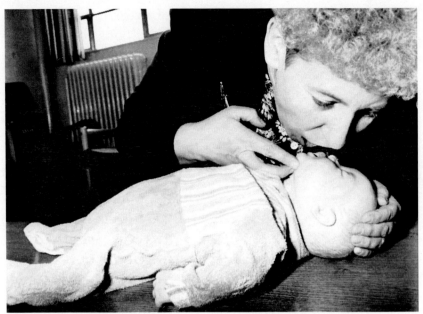
Teaching baby resuscitation to Mother and Baby Groups

My St John career progressed further when I was allowed to form an Adult Combined Division on Bedgrove. Several of the older Cadets joined and some ladies from the church. Over the years we had run short public 'Save a Life' courses on the estate and some of these people around Bedgrove were willing to become members. Colonel Payne, Commandant of Bucks St John Ambulance, gave his blessing and Mrs Maureen Thackray became our President. I had known her from the mental health committees. Bill Bartlett from the hospital treasurer's office became our treasurer.

Training began in earnest. We would also have drill practices and plan our fundraising. Christina Watkins, a new member, was excellent at raising funds and quite soon we were able to purchase an old ambulance from the local ambulance station. This opened up new opportunities for public duties and ambulance aid training. The ambulance was dedicated by the

Vicar of The Church of the Holy Spirit, Bedgrove, with Colonel Payne and Colonel Thomas participating. Some of the local public houses had collecting tins for us and we were allowed a stall outside the shops on Bedgrove for publicity and fundraising. Our flag days were well supported, with each member or a cadet with their parent having two streets allocated to them each June, the nearest week to St John's Day, June 24th. The counting of the tins on the Sunday would often be on one of the hottest days of the year!

Unusually, we had two special families with multiple birth children in St John. Rosemary Crawley had quadruplets, and after our members supported her to help with feeds etc, she helped our Badger group for a number of years and also worked at County Headquarters. Each child was so different from the others and went their own way eventually. The Withers couple, who were in the Adult Division, had triplets and we had a rota to help them. Claire Withers became a trainer for St John Ambulance and Robert a great help with the ambulance and duties. Their son was often a casualty at our exams. Even the Ludlow family had twins, my son Matthew teaching them later on at Bedgrove School. At one time I was nicknamed Miss Bedgrove as I was always around with a different uniform on!

Our second ambulance was bought from Leyland Daf in Birmingham. Derek Flint by that time was in the Ambulance Service and came along to help us. It was rumoured that this was the ambulance used in the ITV series 'London's Burning'. I had concerns about this vehicle as it did not have a passage into the cab, only a sliding side door, but it proved to be a very good vehicle, which became well equipped and was much easier to drive. I was able to acquire the services of the Banbury Police Driving School for several sessions and formed a rota to check the vehicle and take it for a run to keep it maintained.

St John Review magazine sometimes had competitions included when firms donated various pieces of equipment. I entered a

Dedication of Bedgrove's first ambulance, 1986

Getting the ambulance ship-shape!

HRH The Duke of Gloucester opens Tindat Road HQ, 1992

Lady Westbury attends our Presentation Evening, April 1986

competition on the history of the triangular bandage and on resuscitation and won a skill meter Resusci-Anne for the division. This enabled the First Aider to observe the right pressure on chest compressions and correct breaths, and we used it for several displays and publicity days at the local shops. When we moved equipment and meetings from Bedgrove to the new County Headquarters, the recording apparatus disappeared. I never did find out if it was thrown out by mistake, or if someone took it, not really knowing what it was!

Paul was running the Cadet Division and one year we were privileged to have Lady Westbury (Superintendent in Chief) as our guest to present the cups and certificates when she came to visit Bucks St John. We also had a visit from dignitaries and officers from Zimbabwe. Bucks was twinned with Zimbabwe and we would fundraise and send out badges and equipment to them.

Over the years we were able to attend some 'out of county' St John events with special permission. Two years running we went on duty to the large flower festival at Spalding, and another year we took the ambulance to Silverstone. This was a very long day as we left around 5.00 am to be in position at 7.00 am, before the roads were blocked up by the crowds. It was fascinating to observe some dignitaries arriving by helicopter and to view the purpose-built First Aid Station. I found the day very tiring and noisy and fell asleep on my break!

One duty that was very popular over the years was going to Milton Keynes Bowl to provide cover at large pop concerts. Sometimes I was placed in the medical centre and other times in one of the mobile units situated around the perimeter. This was my favourite spot as one could observe the concerts and we were first on the scene of any emergency. In the early days people would want numerous plasters, Paracetamol or ice for stings, but later when it was more established a pharmacy would operate from one of the tents so that people could purchase their

Lord Carrington opens the Croft Road Headquarters, 1981

own packs. Many stalls operated around the perimeter, such as souvenir stalls and refreshment outlets, and we would be given complimentary vouchers for meals and could 'brew up' in the units. I was privileged to see many famous bands and entertainers over the years, Marillion, Metallica, Michael Jackson, Bruce Springsteen and Eminem, to name a few. This also gave the members experience of managing large duties and brought much needed cash into our county funds. Other big duties within the county were The Bucks County Show and Halton Air Show. One year I was on duty at Henley Regatta and another time at an open-air event at Stowe School.

One year Colonel Thomas invited us to the Beating of the Retreat Ceremony at the Army Headquarters and another time we had a duty at Bletchley Park. We attended classic car shows, caravan rallies and duties at Stoke Mandeville sports stadium. There would also be Kimble Point-to-Point on Easter Saturday and Brill Motorbike Scrambles throughout the season. One time a man had a heart attack at Brill and we took him to Stoke Mandeville. This took around 25 minutes. By the time we arrived in Casualty he had used most of the oxygen in the oxygen cylinder. The sister thanked us and said we had kept him going with our care, as it would have been double that time waiting for the ambulance from Stoke Mandeville to drive to Brill.

Another time a man fell from his horse near Brill and had a suspected fractured pelvis. We immobilised him and the local GP came out and administered morphine, and he asked us to use our Entonox cylinder whilst taking him to Stoke Mandeville. One time we were on duty at the Aylesbury Carnival, based at the bottom of the Market Square, when a mother ran down to us carrying her little boy who was choking. I placed him over my lap, tapped his back and a gobstopper was expelled.

Those years were the heyday of public duties, before a lot of private companies started up. At one concert I saw Acker Bilk and at another George Melly. I was on duty at a dance by the Syd Lawrence Orchestra and a Conservative fundraising evening at Winslow with Mrs Thatcher in attendance. From blood donor duties to road races, triathlons, to firework displays, St John was there during all that time.

With the other St John nurses, I was introduced to Lord Carrington when he opened the Croft Road Headquarters, and to the Duke of Gloucester when he opened the Robert Payne County Headquarters and Training Centre in Tindal Road, Aylesbury, in 1992.

As with any division, the make-up changed over the years. It started with mostly older Cadets and ladies from church and progressed to more men joining and further courses on Ambulance Aid, Moving and Handling and Resuscitation techniques using the new Automated External Defibrillators. Many members have contacted me over the years to tell me how useful the Home Nursing Courses were and how they felt

Bedgrove Adults 10th Birthday Party, 1994

confident to look after members of their families, thanks to the practice and tips learnt at the division and also the training to use medical loans equipment, wheelchairs, walkers, back rests and commodes.

Dorothy Simmons and I enjoyed conducting the St John Care Course. This had been modernised from the old Home Nursing. It included body image, sexuality, chronic and acute care, various diets and religious practices, health promotion and rehabilitation. It was taught with vu-foils, using an overhead projector, and the members would use a work book. They produced a project at the end of the course and were encouraged to use the knowledge gained on relatives and friends who became ill in the home. For several years we went to the St John Medical Conference at Nottingham University and other times I went with John to the Care in the Community Conferences organised by Dame Audrey Emerton at hotels in London.

Dot and I examined for a lot of Home Nursing and Care Competitions. I remember competitions at The Grange School, Aylesbury College, Green Park and the old Croft Road Headquarters. We travelled to Shaftesbury, Abingdon and the Ercol Headquarters at Princes Risborough, but the icing on the cake was the National Finals at the Fairfield Halls, Croydon.

We were both keen supporters of the Blood Transfusion Service and Dot and I organised many a rota to send members to help around Bedgrove and Aylesbury. My mother was a supporter and would help at sessions in Bletchley, Milton Keynes and in the Open University Headquarters at Walton. I regularly gave blood and was presented with my gold badge in a ceremony held at Witney in 1998. I managed 67 pints before having to give it up for health reasons.

There were two special duties after the millennium. The first was when HM The Queen visited Higginson Park Marlow on 10th May 2002 to unveil the statue of Olympian Sir Steve

HM The Queen at Marlow, 2002

Redgrave. It was purely luck where you are placed when on duty! You may be very near some VIPs or in a back street to keep an eye on the crowds. This time I was in a mobile unit very close to the royal party and my mother was in the Women's Institute's tent, as a group of elderly care home residents from her care home had been invited to join the proceedings. HRH Prince Philip noticed the medal that my mother was wearing and asked her what it was. She was able to tell him that it was her St John Service Medal.

On 29th November 2007 HM The Queen visited our new headquarters and training centre at Greenleys, Milton Keynes. Her Majesty arrived quite late in a glass-topped Bentley, as her chauffeur had got lost in the city. After she unveiled the plaque and signed the visitors' book, we gave a very realistic First Aid demonstration using plenty of casualty make-up. This ceremony was the culmination of several years hard work and much dedication by John Williams to raise the funds for a modern training centre, suitable for the needs of the 21st century in the expanding city.

Helping with fundraising at the St John Fair in 2007

CHAPTER 16
SPREADING MY WINGS

During the 1990s Community Care was coming to the forefront because of the Government Community Care Act and because Baroness Audrey Emerton DBE DL had been appointed St John Chief Commander nationally. A competition was held for Brigade members to write an essay and the winners would receive a bursary from various firms to aid the work of St John. I wrote an essay on communication and mental health and was surprised when a letter arrived stating that I had won the Smith and Nephew award for £750. I would use the money to study mental health teams in two contrasting parts of the country. The Awards Ceremony was held at St John's Gate, Clerkenwell on 7th June 1994 in the Priory Church. Mrs Yvonne Moores, Chief Nursing Officer, Department of Health would present the Awards following a short interview by the Baroness Emerton.

A Junior Officer from the northwest of the country won an award, as did Nursing Officer Barbara Ninham from Dorchester. Afterwards a reception was held in the Chapter Hall. I had plans to visit a Leicester inner city mental health team and compare how it worked with a rural seaside team in Dorset. Barbara immediately said that I must stay with her, as the team for the elderly mental health was situated in Bridport at the Forston Clinic. My Nursing Officer at the John Hampden Unit, Mr Dave Moore, was very supportive of my plan and helped me arrange the placement at Leicester. I was given two lots of three days for study leave.

Nursing Bursary presented by HRH Duchess of Gloucester, June 1993

The following year I was seconded from my CPN job to undergo the CPN Diploma Course at Nene College, Northampton. After I returned, I was offered a new post in St John, as County Care in the Community Officer, completely voluntary. Community Care projects would be expanded, so what could Buckinghamshire do? I supported the John Hampden's Relatives Support Group and they said a Sitting Service would be beneficial. This was voluntary at first, then after some grants became available, we advertised and appointed twelve sitters for the project and an organiser. Training was held and leaflets printed. Mostly the sitters would read, play board games, watch television or take someone for a walk, whilst the carer went shopping or did a hobby, such as swimming, or bowls. Some carers were able to attend Carers' Training Sessions and one carer went to an evening class. Some clients had dementia, others a learning disability and others some physical disabilities. It was very successful whilst it lasted, only finishing when the grants ran out. This type of service has been taken up by Carers Groups now and Age UK.

John Williams, our County Commander, was very keen that we publicise the 'one-stop shop' where we could point carers in the right direction for services and Dorothy Simmons, County Nursing Officer, expanded the Medical Loans Scheme. We had a store of equipment for loan to carers, such as wheelchairs, backrests, shower stools and walking frames. Another project was to support the Hospital Library Service at County Headquarters by providing a base in which the library volunteers could sort the books and hold spares. I was also involved with carers' training sessions and was on the committees of Aylesbury Vale Carers Association, and along with Mrs Thackray on the local Mind group (Mental Health Charity.) I became County Nursing Officer when Dorothy Simmons left to concentrate on the Fellowship, but several of the St John nurses were retiring and the competitions were discontinued.

I was promoted to Officer Sister in 2000, the Vellum Diploma signed by Dame Audrey Emerton, Chancellor, and I was delighted to see Mrs Margaret Boothman at the ceremony. She came and had a chat afterwards, always looking out for her 'girls from Bucks'. From my SRN Nurses' prize-giving for this award, it had turned full circle!

John and I enjoyed our duties at the Swan Theatre in High Wycombe. The theatre had a family atmosphere with the staff, whom we got to know quite well. 'Prof' from High Wycombe Division and Margaret James would issue the rota for the duty. Our base was the First Aid Room where we were expected to check the stock and the defibrillator. It was luck of the draw what you saw. Sometimes members would swap on the rota if there was something special that they wanted to see. We did not enjoy the Ken Dodd show that went on until 1.00 am, as we had to work the next day! There were a good variety of shows, concerts, bands, comedies and pantomimes. Occasionally we spotted famous people in the audience. Cilla Black came to watch Petula Clark perform, and Warren Clarke from Dalziel and Pascoe came to watch a show one evening.

An unexpected request came for members to provide First Aid cover at Windsor Castle at weekends. Berkshire St John was not able to provide the cover, as they had Ascot Racecourse and other commitments, so for a time Buckinghamshire sent two members at weekends. John and I attended a few times. Our details were sent ahead for security checks and we reported to the main gate in uniform and with our ID. A security guard gave us a private tour of St George's Chapel and the main public areas, then we were shown the First Aid Room and given the emergency arrangements. We checked the defibrillator machine and the equipment and bandages, then spent a very pleasant day observing the public viewing the castle grounds.

As training courses expanded, I would mostly teach the Moving and Handling sessions, Baby Resuscitation, short 'Save a Life' courses, Anaphylactic Shock, Infection Control and Safeguarding. I became an examiner for the then four-day First Aid at Work Examination. In those days the candidates undertook a multi choice question paper, then three scenarios. These would include overall coping with the incident, resuscitation, unconsciousness, a severe bleed and bandaging. I met so many people at these exams from old school mates and ex-Cadets, to people from the local shops and clubs.

I was approached by Richard Kingston from Social Services in 2001 to see if it was feasible to run a Men's Club to support 'difficult to place' men with mental health problems. After my success with day clubs in the villages, he thought Aylesbury would be an ideal location for a small group. The men would be referred from Social Services and the CPN's caseload, as well as open referrals from relatives if appropriate. Some of the ladies who had been involved in the Sitting Service came to help and training was given. Some men had low moods, others memory problems, or chronic mental health problems. We placed an emphasis on physical exercise with chair-based exercises and walks and games sessions in the nearby park. Quizzes and sessions using the flipchart helped with memory and orientation.

We were able to access grants from the Harding Trust, Aylesbury Council and Bucks Community Foundation. The club achieved a very good reputation in the area and continued until the grants dried up and St John altered their priorities to promoting the commercial side in 2012. This was First Aid courses and ambulance work. The Medical Comforts Loan Service was discontinued, Sitting Service and most of the community care work ceased. Many members left the organisation and the smaller halls and headquarters around the county were sold. Nationally the organisation was running at a loss and needed to reorganise. Along with other voluntary organisations, it became more regionalised. The days of

A Monday Club Tea Party

Obtaining grants for the day clubs

volunteer members in rural communities, trained to support their neighbours had finished. The cities and large towns were the priority.

After my adventures abroad I returned to run the Monday Contact Club at the Aylesbury Methodist Church. The club had been put on hold after Janet Neville, the organiser, suffered a stroke. There was still £1,000 kept by the Methodist Church for the club to restart. I spent three happy years as their organiser and three happy years running Waddesdon Wednesday Club, as by that time Kathy Rooke, the organiser, was ready to retire and they wanted me back.

My last occasion in Uniform – at Halton Carol Service with Phillip, 2013

John and I remained in St John as members with the Aylesbury Division until he was 65, when we said goodbye at the division's Christmas Dinner and wrote our resignation letters. The uniform was changing and the volunteer side not really appreciated enough.

We moved to Christchurch, Dorset, in September 2014, purchasing a bungalow, one and a half miles from the beautiful Avon Beach and Mudeford Quay. We remain members of the St John Fellowship Branch in Aylesbury, ably run by Dot and Tony Simmons and a very loyal group of retired members.

Settled in Christchurch

Part 3

CHAPTER 17
A CARE IN THE WORLD

I had always wanted to travel and work abroad. Indeed, when I told my father that I wanted to get married in 1973, he said, "I thought you wanted to use your SRN to nurse abroad?" However, that was not to be for many years. The first opportunity came in 1980 when I was chosen to accompany a group of 16 St John nursing members to Rome for two weeks. It was St John 'Year of Nursing' and the idea was to broaden members knowledge of St John work abroad. I was the trained nurse of the group and we were led by an Area Staff Officer. We assisted and observed the work carried out by nuns in a hospital for patients suffering with paraplegia or strokes. This was in the Magliana Hospital just outside Rome.

St John Year of Nursing to Rome, 1980

Some members were fortunate to be placed at the Eye Hospital in Jerusalem, including my friend, Peter Lymbery, some at a hospital in Aberdeen, Scotland, and three members even went on the QE2 ship. I was probably chosen for the Rome trip because I trained at Stoke Mandeville. This was an unusual opportunity for members of the Protestant British Venerable Order of St John to be invited to the Catholic Order's Hospital.

I was grateful to Roger Titley, the St John President, for this experience. Having just had two weeks' leave, this opportunity arose and he managed to speak to my superiors for me to have another two weeks off, albeit without pay. It would also be very hot in July. Sheila Puckle from National Headquarters and an ex-Army administrator organised the placements, the hotel and the transport each day to the hospital. She also arranged for us to have two grey nurses' dresses and four aprons. We would work in two groups on alternate days from 7.00 am – 2.00 pm. The other day would be free to explore Rome. The hotel was in the centre of Rome with a typical courtyard and Italian menu. As an officer, I was given my own room.

I found the hospital way behind Stoke Mandeville in the care of spinal patients. The patients suffered bedsores and infections, and family members came into the wards to give the basic care such as washes, oral hygiene and meals. Some even stayed by the side of the bed. Medicines were still administered from a medicine cupboard and put on a trolley. Physiotherapy and Occupational Therapy were very sparse. One of the main problems was the language barrier – we didn't speak Italian and they couldn't understand English, so a lot of the time we could only observe and use hand gestures and body language. It certainly made me appreciate our National Health Service.

Off duty made up for the poor nursing experience. National Headquarters managed to obtain tickets for the Pope's regular audience in St Peter's Square with a good view of Pope John Paul II. We were also able to visit his summer retreat at Castel

Gandolfo. Another day the Catholic Sovereign Military Order of St John took us on a visit to their headquarters on the Aventine Hill, which was a great privilege. We were shown the Aventine Church and the Council Chamber where the Knights hold their important meetings. Outside, looking through the beech tree lined avenue, is one of the finest views of St Peter's and Rome. Many of the Knights are from European Nobility and support numerous humanitarian projects around the world.

Visiting St Peter's, the Vatican and the Sistine Chapel when it was quiet, proved to be a wonderful opportunity not possible on package holidays. The Vatican houses the earliest complete Bible, a 4th century parchment known as the Codex Vaticanus, amongst many other treasures. The art, beauty and atmosphere made a great impression and stayed with me for a long time. I became friendly with Doris Goody a member from Westgate Division, in Kent. We explored the famous buildings and monuments of Rome and booked a visit to the Trevi Fountains and a day trip to Capri.

Travelling broadens the mind and educates better than any schooling. Unfortunately, it is addictive, and I was set on the road to try other experiences with St John. My next opportunity came in January 1997 when Roger Barrell MVO, a member of the St John Medical Board, wanted to run a goodwill visit to Pakistan. He had been a member of the Queen's Protection Unit and had many contacts abroad. He advertised in the national St John Review magazine for medical personnel interested in partaking in a trip to Karachi to train the local Civil Defence Corps and Sea Captains. I applied and was successful. Our group consisted of three nurses and three doctors. Roger only agreed to the project if the Pakistan authorities treated the women members as equal trainers. We all paid our own flights and Roger obtained funding to pay for the accommodation. The three females shared a room. Roger had his own room and the other two men shared a room. The hotel was three-star, ex-colonial and had grand pillars at the entrance. The menu was western enough to be tolerable.

We managed to give basic First Aid training to several groups. We had a male nurse who was a hospital resuscitation officer so he gave that training. I mainly demonstrated the recovery position for unconsciousness and the control of severe bleeding from the arm and leg. Like many places abroad the participants didn't like to touch the casualty, but gradually with smiles and goodwill we overcame it.

I became friendly with Pat Morris, a nursing officer from Hampshire, and we managed to explore a little of Karachi when off duty. We had a public health doctor who tried to be too theoretical and impart all his knowledge and this was annoying when we were trying to teach the basics in a different language and culture. It was important to teach what the group wanted and not what the teacher could impress them with. However, it was a good grounding for other placements abroad. The final member of the team was a medical student from Northern Ireland.

Although the rooms were equipped with fans, it was still very overpowering to teach First Aid. We all suffered from 'Delhi belly' during the ten days, so mostly the group was five out of six personnel. Toiletries, First Aid training equipment and school materials were taken out to be distributed to some children's homes. The Oral B company sent me a large box of toothbrushes and toothpaste for distribution, and I had a tombola at The Grange School Fete to raise money for charity goods.

The St John officers in Karachi organised several visits for us. One was a dinner at the Royal Karachi Sailing Club. They served a very hot curry and I put most of it in paper napkins under the table when possible! Another was a visit along the coast for a barbecue and paddle at dusk. We travelled in convoy with the St John Karachi officers in the back and front

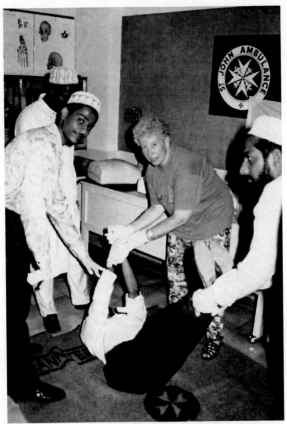

Teaching First Aid in Karachi

minibuses and us in the middle minibus. They were very conscious of security even in those days. We were not allowed to swim and were required to keep our arms and legs covered. We also had to hand in our cameras as the authorities were very security conscious there.

The worst visit was to the port area and a very smelly fish market by the docks. There was also a huge open laundry by the river and estuary, that was also very smelly. One day we were taken to a large city market to observe how their teenage male members undertook First Aid duties. They were equipped with walkie talkies and manned several First Aid posts across the area.

We were made honorary scouts one evening when we visited a large scout group that played a band. Another evening we had a meeting with the British Consul and his wife in the consulate building. On entering the compound, our minibus was checked underneath for explosives, using a mirror on a long pole. The consul's wife was obviously experienced in putting on receptions and it was a lovely meal in cool air-conditioned surroundings.

Pakistan forbids drinking, so it is very difficult to purchase alcohol legally. When the doctors fancied a drink, they asked the hotel manager for the procedure. Later that evening the manager brought us a bottle of gin. The paperwork for this bottle was incredible. We were allowed the drink because we were foreigners and tourists, but special papers were completed by filling in forms in triplicate. The staff had no idea how to pour the drinks, so when a large quantity was poured, we kept topping it up with lemonade.

One of the senior St John officers, Mr Abdul Shakoor, took us out to tea to meet his grandchildren. He was such a gentle, pleasant man and it provided a welcome relief from the formal sessions. I did meet him a year or two later when he came to England for the St Paul's Annual Dedication Service.

The next opportunity for teaching abroad came in 2001, as Buckinghamshire St John was twinned with St John in Zimbabwe. We began to fundraise and send them equipment. Uniforms, badges, blankets, and First Aid materials were gladly received. Over the years Bucks sent two ambulances full of stores to Zimbabwe.

Bobby Massey and Margaret James, our county trainers, went to Zimbabwe and ran courses in 'training the trainer' so that the St John in Harare and Bulawayo were skilled and up to date. They could then provide training to their members and members of the public. Offices and factories would send employees for training. This provided revenue for St John.

Having met Ting Edmonstone, the country's St John Nursing Officer, and the Commissioner, Gerry Sibanda, I put out feelers to see if they would like some four-day nursing courses based on our new Caring for the Sick Manual. Again, it would help their members get up to date and they could market the course to health care assistants and members of the public. Margaret Finn, the National Administrator, arranged a lovely programme for John and me. We spent five days in Harare for the first course and then moved to Bulawayo for another course. John endured three bed baths and was sent out for drinks, supplies and paper towels. He also helped Ting with a school First Aid exam and ambulance work.

*Ting and Gerry over to visit us from Zimbabwe
for our twinning, with John Williams*

Afterwards, we travelled to Victoria Falls to see a little of the country by train and witness the breath-taking Victoria Falls. The country was just starting to experience petrol shortages, so we were not able to visit the Great Zimbabwe ruins or Cecil Rhodes' grave. We did manage to witness the ancient rock paintings and see the huge Lake Chivero that provides hydroelectric power and water for Harare. In Bulawayo, whilst I was teaching, John was able to go on ambulance duty and was taken to the large railway headquarters, where he visited Cecil Rhodes' train carriage and saw a cheque written by Rhodes preserved on a wall plaque. It was entirely self-funded, but the staff did show us an amazing mock English Tudor building and a game lodge restaurant for meals. At lunch time we would have filled rolls, but the Zimbabwe members fried some insects. Stephen, the caretaker used the stove and explained to us that the poor people ate the insects for protein. He would cook maize, beef and dried caterpillars!

I asked the members to be ready for the training at 8.30 am as I was told that in Zimbabwe time they would probably arrive for 9.00 am. We used an overhead projector and vu foils for teaching and each member was given a Caring for the Sick book. Ting was insistent that we gave them a test and certificate at the end of the course. The only difference in the teaching was that thermometers could not be placed in the mouth as the HIV/Aids epidemic was increasing. We also provided training on abuse and rights, as they explained to me about men called 'sugar daddies' who preyed on youngsters. We left videos and a lot teaching materials for them and we held an Aids/HIV awareness afternoon, when over fifty pupils from a school came to the St John Hall for training. Mr Patel, one of my pharmacy contacts in Aylesbury, gave me a large box of condoms, but teenagers being teenagers, I wonder how much of the seriousness of the condition was heeded?

Molly, the Area Superintendent, took us to the Bulawayo Bowls Club and the Cricket Club where we met expats. I wonder how they managed later on as conditions deteriorated? Molly and Gerry took us to the Chipangali Animal Orphanage where we viewed, among other animals, a white rhino and a cheetah.

The staff saw us off from Bulawayo station on the overnight train and we slept on couchettes. The next morning, we arrived at Victoria Falls. The marvellous five-star Victoria Falls Hotel adjoins the railway station. At the bottom of the hotel garden we could see the spray and hear the 'smoke that thunders'. There was a clear view of the falls, Zambezi River and the 200-metre bridge. The old colonial hotel was marvellous with first class service and lush gardens. Whilst there we undertook a ride across the border to Zambia to see the largest falls in the world from the other side. We also visited the first school, hospital and museum. The museum in Livingstone contained relics and information about David Livingstone. Another highlight was the booze cruise. This is a boat ride at 6.00 pm to witness the beautiful sunset and animals by the Zambezi River. Alcoholic drinks and canapes were served. We saw several hippopotami, monkeys, giraffes and elephants. We were sad to fly home, via Harare, as everyone had made us very welcome.

Just after we arrived home, a letter arrived from a young lady in Harare. Linda Kutukwa had heard about our visit, as her friend had been on our course. She badly wanted to come to Britain to study with St John in order to improve her chances of hospital work. She had already undertaken some voluntary work at Harare Hospital and I advised her to wait until she was 18 and we would investigate if it were possible to stay with us and have some training with Buckinghamshire St John. The rest is history.

Linda came and lived with us for nine months. She was the daughter that I never had. She undertook many training courses and duties with us and gained experience in the day clubs and community work. Gloria, the Matron, gave her work at Bartlett's Care Home and eventually she met Paul through

The Kutukwa Family – Linda with her parents

St John, who was to become her husband and they have a son, Phillip, who is a joy.

We did not know the procedure if she wanted to stay permanently in Britain, so after consultation with the Member of Parliament and their local vicar, Linda went with Paul to Zimbabwe and completed the documents from there. Much success followed. Linda gained her British Citizenship and I was thrilled to attend the ceremony in the Judges' Lodgings in Aylesbury. She passed her driving test and went to Aylesbury College to gain the qualifications required for University. She is now an Occupational Therapist, having qualified from Northampton University, and John and I attended the graduation ceremony on the hottest day of 2019!

Linda's Citizenship ceremony at the Judges' Lodgings, 2013

Chapter 18
Pilgrimages

'Pilgrimage'. The dictionary defines this as 'a journey to a sacred place'. It is different from a holiday as it is to study, reflect and co-operate with fellow pilgrims. You don't choose your fellow travellers and believers. God asked Abraham to go in search of the promised land, so he became the first pilgrim as he went in faith and obedience. (Genesis 12 v 1-9) The Eastern Orthodox Church tends to use icons to aid their devotions. The Catholic Church uses relics and statues, and like the Protestant faithful visit religious places 'In the Footsteps of Christ'.

Walsingham

One of the most important shrines in England is at Walsingham, Norfolk, and is often nicknamed England's Nazareth. Walsingham became a shrine after a reputed apparition reported by Richeldis de Faverches, a Saxon noblewoman in 1061. She was told by the Virgin Mary to build a replica of the Holy Family's house in Nazareth. This was to be in honour of the Annunciation. Henry VIII dissolved the two monastic houses there during the Reformation. In 1897, Pope Leo XIII decreed the refounding of the 14 century Slipper Chapel. Two decades later, Father Alfred Hope Patten revived the pilgrimage for Anglicans. The shrine called Our Lady of Walsingham was completed in 1938.

John and I were invited to visit the shrine in 2003. St Barnabas Church, Linslade, Bedfordshire was where Nesta Warren, our St John friend, worshipped. They were undertaking a pilgrimage weekend. The members were High Church Anglicans and this came across in the services and hymns. Processions, vigils and readings were held in the red brick 1930s buildings. On our arrival, one lady made me laugh – she wanted to check Nesta's friends and asked us if we were actually married!

The accommodation was of a basic hostel type, but the grounds were beautifully presented for meditation and processions. Pilgrims come to receive blessings and to celebrate the Eucharist. Its tranquil surroundings were ideal for prayer and reflection. Many pilgrims feel united in their beliefs and it deepens their connection to God. It was an uplifting experience.

Lourdes, France

I undertook my next pilgrimage later that year when Margaret Fielding, one of our St John nurses from High Wycombe, invited me to accompany her and her group of disabled members to Lourdes for a week in August. It was the annual Northampton Diocese Pilgrimage, travelling with the Catholic Association Pilgrimage Trust. Margaret required more nurses to support the patients. My flight and accommodation would be paid and in return I would help in the care of her group. She recruited three more nurses, Elaine, Myrna and Anna.

We set off in a very old aeroplane to Lourdes, France. I was surprised to see Bella at the airport, who was a nurse on the John Hampden Wards at Stoke Mandeville Hospital, as I had no idea that she helped with the Lourdes Pilgrimages. The Hotel Beau was situated centrally on the banks of the River Gave. I shared a room with another nurse. The food was very basic, including a continental breakfast and snack lunch. After helping pilgrims first thing each morning I would go into the town and purchase a meal in one of the many restaurants! Some visit Lourdes purely as a tourist site amidst the beautiful Pyrenees mountains and others for spiritual health. Many find that they are able to accept their illnesses and face life's challenges better after this stay.

Pilgrimage to Lourdes, 2003

The story of Lourdes is wonderful. Bernadette Soubirous was born to a poor family of millers from Lourdes in 1844. On 11th February 1858 Bernadette went with her sister and friend to collect dead wood along the banks of the River Gave. As she walked by the rocks and caves, she saw an apparition of a lady in white. Bernadette knelt down and said her rosary prayer and the lady disappeared. She asked her companions if they had noticed anything, but they said they had not.

On the third apparition she was told to visit every day for two weeks. Gradually more people went with Bernadette to witness her state of ecstasy at the grotto. A spring appeared on the ninth apparition and has increased in volume and is now the source of the famous baths at Lourdes. On the thirteenth apparition the message was given to her that the priests should have a chapel built there. Later, at the sixteenth apparition, the figure told Bernadette that she was the 'Immaculate Conception'. This was a strange remark for an uneducated 14-year-old girl to take in. This statement refers to the conception of Mary that she was born without original sin so had a special moral purity to give a virgin birth. The priests then recognised the vision that appeared had to be the Virgin Mary. The last apparition was on 16th July 1858; her state of ecstasy lasted about fifteen minutes when the lady in white said goodbye.

On 15th July 1860 Bernadette entered a hospice run by the Sisters of Nevers. After taking the veil on 30th October 1867 she stayed with the sisters for about 12 years in the convent, but was plagued with bouts of asthma. She had an asthmatic attack on 16th April 1879 and died at the age of 35. The area became a holy site with many churches and religious buildings being built. Now over five million pilgrims visit Lourdes every year.

The three huge churches in the centre are known as the Basilica and are on different levels. There were various services each day – one was in the modern round rotunda Saint Bernadette Church built in 1988. The service I found most moving was at the end of the candlelight procession. The candles, torchlights and lanterns lit up the procession as it weaved its way along the riverbank to the grotto, where the service took place. At some services oil was used for healing and, at others, holy water. We were very unfortunate with the weather as it was drizzly and misty. I wore my Danimac over my white nursing dress most days.

On the Monday we all congregated for a group photograph with the Bishop of Northampton. Later that day Margaret Fielding showed us around the Accueil Notre-Dame and Accueil Marie Saint Frai. These hospital-type buildings have been completely modernised and can accommodate up to 1,300 people. The rooms contain up to six beds and have been designed to encourage people to meet one another. There are duty doctors and nurses here throughout the 24 hours.

On the Tuesday we were taken by coach into the Pyrenees to a town called Gavarnie. As the weather improved, we could see that it was a winter skiing resort and we viewed a waterfall and the hydroelectric power station. The pretty Edelweiss flowers were in bloom and we went past a thermal spring resort. This outing gave us a greater appreciation of the area.

Another day I helped a lady, disabled with arthritis, to go to the baths. The 16 baths were constructed in 1955 and many people bathe there every day – the water is completely changed every 24 hours. She was helped to undress and gown up and was dipped into the water. We then helped her dress. In the northern part of the Basilica there are the drinking taps fed from the spring. My main patient to look after suffered from chronic depression and I feel that she did benefit from the experience of going to Lourdes.

One day I went with another nurse to visit buildings connected to Bernadette. We visited the Boly Mill where the family lived when Bernadette was born. Another dwelling is the Cachot, a small room that had been used formerly as a jail. They lived here in extreme poverty when they were evicted from the mill.

Father Peyramale, the local priest, rented the Maison Paternelle in 1863 for the family (there were four children) when he could see the dreadful conditions they were living in at the Cachot. This was a much better building and had a mill. It was Father Peyramale that supported Bernadette when she confided in him that it was the Immaculate Conception that she was seeing.

There was a land train that took people to the tourist sites which was very useful. The sites included a model village of Lourdes, an audio-visual display, a museum and a nativity display. It was also possible to visit a chateau fort and ride on a funicular up the hill for a panoramic view of the area. Everywhere around the location various Ave Maria music was played.

At the end of the trip Margaret gave us a special prayer card each and later that month invited John and me to her house for a meal. She works hard each year to find the nurses required to enable the trip to take place. It was certainly a worthwhile experience where I saw and experienced another side of life for chronically ill people.

CHAPTER 19

THE ORDER OF ST JOHN EYE HOSPITAL
JERUSALEM

For many years it had been my ambition to serve at the Order of St John Hospital in Jerusalem. The chance finally came when I stood down from the John Hampden Unit. I mentioned to Margaret Boothman DStJ that this was my aim on finishing work with the health service. I believe Roy Mercer also put a word in for me; his wife had been our County Superintendent previously and he was the Hospital Representative for Kent at that time and I spoke to him when they were attending the annual retirement party at Tindal Road held each August.

I wrote to the Hospital's office in London and eventually was requested to attend for an interview. The Hospitaller, Professor Anthony Chignell, was in attendance and also Miss Emblin the ex-Matron who had recently retired from Moorfields Eye Hospital, which is twinned with the Jerusalem Hospital, and was now helping St John. Miss Emblin kindly recommended some ophthalmic books for me to read and I was fortunate to gain permission to observe the ophthalmology clinics and operations by Mr Benjamin, the senior surgeon of the Ophthalmology Department at Stoke Mandeville Hospital. The Matron of the St John Eye Hospital in Jerusalem Jackie Jaidy, wrote to me advising what to bring and saying that they would pay for my flights and nursing insurance. As I was not ophthalmic trained, she suggested that I help in the recovery room of the theatres and give training sessions on First Aid in the School of Nursing. The staff were expected to take an annual re-examination on the priorities of First Aid and I would be under the direction of Ahmad Ma'ali, the Nurse Tutor.

On 6th November 2005 I flew to Ben Gurion Airport for my six-month experience. The adventure had begun. A hospital driver met me at the airport to take me to the hospital and as it was a Sunday the hospital was very quiet. I was shown the flat in the sisters' quarters and left to settle in. Matron had left me some basic provisions in the kitchen refrigerator. I was given a large twin-bedded room opposite a bathroom. It was a large flat with two bathrooms, a kitchen and TV lounge. The cable TV had the History Channel, BBC World and movie channels. I would share this accommodation with Ahmad and a night sister.

Steve James was the hospital CEO at the time and was on a three-year placement from Britain. He came and introduced himself and gave me a lift down the road to the old city, so that I could explore some of the area that day.

The staff started work at 7.00 am and worked until 2.00 pm when it would get very hot. Many of the staff spent a lot of time at the checkpoints to gain entry into East Jerusalem from e.g. Bethlehem, Bethany, or Ramallah, as they needed to cross the separation wall. This can take an hour or two making the working day much longer.

I reported to Matron's office the next morning at 9.00 am. She gave me a white tunic to wear and a black cardigan for the cooler weather. I was given a tour of the hospital then settled into the Sir Stephen Millar School of Nursing to plan the First Aid timetable with Ahmad. The School of Nursing consisted of a practical room, library and classroom. The nine-month course is linked to Moorfields Hospital and Thames University.

Upon completion, graduates were awarded a Postgraduate Diploma in Ophthalmic Nursing, accredited by the University of West London. The library had many interesting books, not just on eye care, but on Palestine and the Middle East. A regular magazine that I was able to read was the publication called Bridges, an Israeli-Palestinian Public Health Magazine that used studies and research from both countries to work together. It is

Ahmad Ma'ali, now CEO Director

sponsored by the World Health Organisation with the paradigm 'Health as a Bridge for Peace'. Its aim is to build relationships, links and common understanding between the two communities of health care professionals.

Some afternoons I would read books under the lovely orange trees. The hospital gardener kept the gardens immaculate and they were a place of calm and comfort for relatives waiting for their family. The hospital building was built on three levels and opened in 1960. Some of the areas were no longer used, as many patients are treated as day cases, or seen at clinic. Three wards were in use – male, female and the children's ward. There was a large orthoptic department, where children were seen that suffer from squints, and the outpatient department was quite noisy and busy. I was also shown the laundry and CSSD department for sterilising equipment; upstairs was a research centre and a room for making artificial eyes. Between 2000-2004, 33 people had their eyes removed and required artificial eyes. I was shown the doctors' study room and a large conference hall. I was invited to use the senior staffroom for breaks and coffees and I started a book swapping shelf here, which proved popular.

Coffee Break with Nursing Sisters Meg and Ann

I also spent time with the other senior nursing sisters, Ann Zawahreh and Meg Digsby. They had trained at Manchester Eye Hospital and married Palestinians and eventually settled in Jerusalem. Patients were given a good meal at lunchtime with a hot main course and usually an orange for dessert. A stall holder outside the hospital sold the traditional foods of falafel and chickpea balls dipped in humous, which we would have on our coffee breaks.

"As-salaam alaikum" ("Peace be upon you") is what the students would greet me with and taught me to say. Training sessions went quite well with approximately eight to ten attending each time. I had brought gauze, various bandages and teaching materials out with me and the hospital had a resuscitation model (Resuci- Anne). There was a flipchart and I made some charts. The staff spoke excellent English and some of the nurses held two degrees. Eight nurses were undertaking the six-month post graduate eye course and I was able to give them some sessions on health and safety, moving and handling, fire safety and

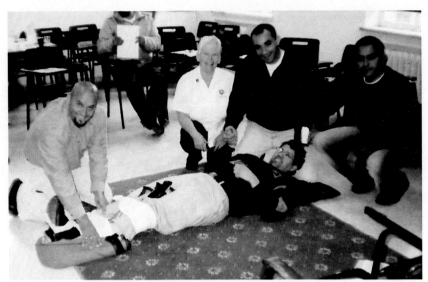

Training Staff at the Jerusalem Eye Hospital

depression. Poverty and unemployment are rife in the West Bank so a session on depression was useful to the students. Matron attended the fire safety session with 21 other nurses, as the sprinkler system for the hospital had just been completed. The video clip that I brought demonstrated to them how quickly a fire can spread.

The second part of my remit was to help in the recovery room of the operating theatre. Matron's husband, Khalid Jaidy, was in charge of the theatres. I became friendly with the two anaesthetists. They had to learn Russian so that they could go to Russia to study and become anaesthetists. I was full of admiration for them. They both enjoyed going into the desert to study the stars with their telescopes.

I was expected to stay with the young children and help keep them still on the theatre trolleys so that they didn't roll off. I also took the observations in the recovery area, such as blood pressures, pulse and oxygen levels. Two operating theatres were used Monday to Friday. One had a list of four to six cataract operations to perform and the other squint corrections, vitrectomies and longer operations. Each theatre had an anaesthetist and a technician, an operating surgeon, and another doctor who was being taught. There were the sterile nurses and the dirty nurses for each theatre, and two nurses setting up equipment and liaising with CSSD, with another nurse in the wash room.

There were two nurses and two porters in the recovery area. Another two nurses came on duty at 2.00 pm to cover emergencies. Everyone helped with the cleaning of the theatres, and the operating list was produced the day before so that equipment could be prepared. The infection rate was very low at the hospital – five cases in 1,900 operations in 2003, and nine cases over 2,807 operations in 2005. This rate is closely monitored and is half the rate of that in Europe. I was able to watch many operations on a TV monitor in each theatre. A lot of high-tech computer equipment is used. Sometimes medical students from other hospitals came to watch procedures. The

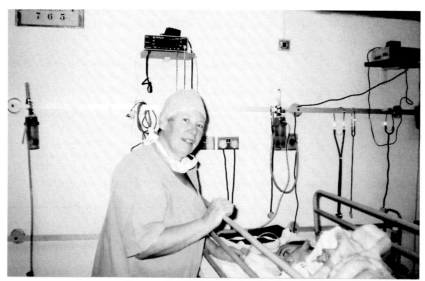

Recovery area in the Eye Hospital

turnover of patients now is much greater than years ago as most patients only stay overnight, compared to 3-4 days several years previously. Over 250 operations are performed in the theatres every month, with laser surgery carried out in the outpatients clinic.

Over the months I was able to find a niche for myself to serve the hospital. The first opportunity came just before Christmas. A carol service was held at St George's Cathedral the Anglican Church in East Jerusalem. Many local Christians, expats and consulate staff came with their children and a collection was taken. Parents gave very generously, as the money raised was for the hospital children's wards. Father Christmas appeared after the service in the refectory, to give a small present to each child and refreshments were served. Steve James asked me if I would be one of the collectors for the service. At the appropriate part of the service I went around the congregation and everyone else, even the choir and servers! Steve James was very pleased afterwards that we had collected £750, the most they had ever raised!

My supporters at home raised some money. Phyl Saw, my day club organiser and friend, held a fete in her garden before I left. £800 was presented to Matron on my arrival. Matron used it to purchase some new equipment for the CSSD department. Some friends sent me £50 for the hospital, and the wards purchased some plastic garden chairs for the visitors on the wards to use.

The nearby British Consulate staff wanted an update on First Aid so I gave an afternoon on First Aid priorities to twelve of their staff. One of their staff was very well informed and knew that the resuscitation number had been altered to thirty compressions and two breaths before it came into our St John First Aid Book! They gave a generous donation.

An Ophthalmic Conference was held at the hospital with delegates from other hospitals in the area paying to attend. They wanted to update on the latest research and treatment, as St John is one of the leading eye hospitals in the Middle East. Around 60 delegates attended and I was able to man the reception desk and assist with making the day run smoothly. Earlier the Hospitaller, Judith Hoburn from New Zealand, and her husband, had been at the hospital and painted and decorated the large conference room voluntarily, to show some support from the members of New Zealand who run the ambulance service there. They treated the staff to a lunch held in the hospital gardens, serving roast lamb which was the special dish. Judith invited me to accompany her on a visit to the site of the previous eye hospital, now Mt Zion Hotel. Another time Professor Chignall paid a visit when I was just clearing up in one of the classrooms. He was keen to know how the placement was going and I was able to tell him some of my experiences.

I hadn't been at the hospital long when an Investiture was held to present some staff with long service awards and to promote some

Lord Vestey GCStJ at the Dinner after the Investiture

to the Order. Lord Vestey KCVO DL, as Chairman of the board, and some other members came from England. The ceremony and meal afterwards was held in the Ambassador Hotel.

Whilst the guests were visiting, they went to the new clinic at Hebron and officially opened it. This serves a population of 600,000 residents. This area is particularly affected by the movement restrictions in the West Bank. The building was previously a private maternity hospital, but it didn't pay when the government opened one up. The clinic was spacious, well decorated and the rooms had been well adapted for various roles – vision tests, laser, orthoptics, theatres, recovery, medical records and a reception area, to name but a few.

I returned to Hebron with Matron a few months later and was amazed by how busy it had become. Another clinic was opened at Anabta to relieve patients having to travel to Jerusalem. They find it hard to obtain the money to travel and very difficult to get permission to go through the separation wall. Ten years later, in 2016, Hebron Hospital treated 13,600 patients and performed over 500 major eye surgeries, and the Anabta Clinic treated over 21,000 patients. Many patients are referred by the Palestinian Authority and others by the United Nations World Relief Authority (UNWRA).

Some of the staff asked me if I would provide some First Aid training to their children. Jerusalem can be a dangerous place with uneven pavements, chaotic traffic and security incidents. A First Aid Club was started every Wednesday afternoon when they came out of school. Some understood English more than others, but I was able to explain with quiz sheets and handouts, and one girl helping with interpreting. Numbers would vary – sometimes only five children and another time eleven. They were keen to practise the bandaging and were soon able to try some mock incidents. One Wednesday we set up a mock road accident in the car park and another day an accident with a fall down some steps outside Matron's office! A week or two later, a boy fell and broke his arm, so his brother was able to help him and they came and proudly showed me his plaster.

One patient who sticks in my memory is a 20-year-old girl who had congenital cataracts. Many families inter-marry and this makes them more prone to health problems. She could not get married as she could not see to run a household. Both eyes were operated on and I was able to witness when the bandages were removed on the ward. It was amazing as she was slowly able to look around and distinguish shapes. The girl would now be able to be independent and undertake tasks impossible previously.

Another girl came to the ward. She was very large with big hands and feet, her colouring was white, and she had an albino genetic make-up. After her operation the staff had quite a job to move and assist her. This was when I was able to give my moving and handling training sessions. Matron noted that people are getting bigger generally and made the decision to order some bigger beds.

Some of the staff's relatives required operations and I remember a nurse using a side room for one of the sister's husbands when he needed a cataract operation. One little toddler belonging to a member of staff was amazed to be able to see clearly once his bandage was removed. It brought a tear to my eyes when I was observing these patients.

I remember observing two little toddlers in the orthoptist clinic. These twins both had squints and needed special glasses to correct their eyes. Their father brought them to clinic regularly for check-ups.

The orthoptists use little toys and figures to check how the child looks across at moving figures. I was able to send a box of suitable little toys, amazingly from the Roald Dahl Museum at Great Missenden! Many toys are donated to the Children's Ward and clinics. Some are given to the children as they are very poor and do not have many toys. I witnessed boys making a ball from rubber bands and toys from twigs.

Some clinics are for patients suffering from glaucoma (pressure building up at the back of the eye), some for damage and injury to the eye and others for diabetic neuropathy. Many Palestinians don't realise that they have developed diabetes. This in turn affects the eyes and sight becomes damaged. Medication and control of blood pressure is required if they are to preserve their eyesight. Poverty, genetics, lifestyle and access to healthcare, all play a part in making blindness ten times higher there than in the West.

Some eminent Israeli doctors lent their support to the hospital, despite the political differences. Professor Mirren from the prestigious 2,000-bed Hadassah Hospital often came to the eye hospital to perform the more complicated operations. He was a prominent Israeli surgeon, upholding the motto of St John to treat anyone regardless of race, creed or colour. Another Israeli surgeon was a lady from Ashkelon (an old Canaanite city, the birthplace of Herod the Great) who came once a week to operate. I also met an Ophthalmic surgeon from Malta – he was a Knight of the Sovereign Military Order and came to help on a short placement.

One remarkable family were the Da la Ruch family of medics from New York. They had visited the hospital for over ten years and given up annual leave to operate at the hospital for a fortnight per year. They brought five cases of equipment with them. Patients requiring plastic surgery would be collected for them, as they operated on the muscles around the eye, reconstruction of the eye socket, growths around the eye lids, removal of cysts and eye troubles from the eye to the nose. The wife was a theatre sister, another member was a nurse tutor and another a physician. This incredible family operated Monday to Friday, then went along to the Dead Sea resorts to relax for the weekend and returned to operate for a second week before returning to America. Their casual happy disposition, whilst working in theatre, was amazing. The young Nick Sergeant from Britain was the whiz kid for cataracts. He worked very fast and trained many junior doctors on his cataract removal technique.

At Easter I joined Steve James and some of the Christian staff for an Easter Egg hunt on the Mount of Olives. Ann James, his wife, had brought a picnic, and whilst some of the children were searching for the hard-boiled eggs I spoke to some American ladies who said they were nuns. They were in skirts and blouses, not nuns' habits. They were called 'peace angels' and their mission was to take medication, parcels and scarce goods into the West Bank and occupied territories. As Americans they were allowed past the separation wall and took drugs for people who had cancer or required special equipment that the Palestinians could not fetch. One had been a nun since 1948, the other since 1974. They helped children cross the wall to attend special schools and would also visit and stay with prisoners.

I also met the Director of the American YMCA building from West Jerusalem; he was on a placement for three years. Speaking about saving money, he said in a typical American drawl, "It's not what you earn girl, it's what of it you manage to keep that counts." He invited me back to the YMCA building opposite the King David Hotel in West Jerusalem to see some traditional Jewish dancing.

Over the years many members of the Royal Family have paid a visit to the eye hospital, including Prince Philip in the 1950s, and Princess Alice of Gloucester in 1961, who was the mother of Richard, our Grand Prior. Prince William also recently visited on his tour of Jerusalem and Bethlehem.

Footnote

Back home, at the County AGM held in the Aylesbury Civic Centre the following year, I was presented with a Commendation for my work at the St John Eye Hospital. It had been sent from the Eye Hospital Headquarters in London unbeknown to me! Mrs Boothman was in the audience and had a lovely chat to me afterwards about the experience.

CHAPTER 20
THE OLD CITY

The Old City of Jerusalem is divided into four quarters, so on my visits I concentrated on one part each day after work. The Jewish Quarter has several houses that are museums telling Jewish history, and excavations can be seen of ruins dating from the Roman occupation. Remains of the Roman-Byzantine Cardo (the main street), which lie below today's street level, can also be viewed. Thousands of visitors from all over the world visit the Western Wall or Wailing Wall and it gets very crowded. I found a path further back that overlooks the wall and gives the best view of the pilgrims praying.

The Arab Quarter is crowded, busy and noisy and the markets display such a wide range of products. On a Saturday morning I would wander along the bazaars to look at the fascinating array of goods. One day I purchased some face powder and coat hangers, and on another day I found a cobbler to mend my sandals. At that time there had been more trouble between the Israelis and Palestinians and security was tight. I found that I could only visit the El-Aksa Mosque and the Temple Mount area on a Tuesday afternoon. This is the large silver-domed mosque constructed in the 8th century by Caliph Walid. As a non-Muslim, I was only allowed to walk around the grounds and buildings and not be allowed into the mosque. There are many shrines on the Temple Mount associated with Mohammed, also fountains where the Muslims wash their feet before prayer. The Jews regard the Dome of the Rock as the place where the ark containing the Ten Commandments was kept. It was the temple where Jesus went to worship and celebrated the Feast of the Passover. Underneath the Temple Mount are subterranean vaults called Solomon's Stables; here the crusaders kept their horses. The panoramic view from the Table Mount is impressive, and providing one was quiet and respectful it was fine to wander around undisturbed.

One afternoon I visited the Armenian Quarter. This area is small but the old city has had Armenians living in it since 300 AD. There is the magnificent Church of St James; this is dedicated to St James the Apostle and also St James the brother of Jesus. (Mark 6 v3). He led the early church in Jerusalem whilst St Paul was preaching to the Gentiles. At the side of the church is a small museum telling the details of the genocide of Armenians by the Ottoman Turks during the First World War. The Armenians appeared to be a gentle people and two of the nurses who worked at the hospital were Armenian.

The Christian Quarter by comparison is quite large and it was easy to get lost down the narrow paths. The main street of the Via Dolorosa (meaning the Way of the Cross) has many shops and stalls and memorials along it. These commemorate the final journey of Jesus carrying the cross. Many pilgrims like to go along it on a Friday, and at Easter the monks process along. Two celebrations of Easter are held, one by the Western Church and another by the Eastern Orthodox Church depending on calendar dates.

One of the doctors introduced me to the Austrian Hospice, which overlooks the main Via Dolorosa Square. I was taken through a gate and up some steps into a corridor that led to a restaurant. This was a lovely place for refreshment either inside or in the elevated garden. It also served as a hostel to stay in and I was taken upstairs to the roof to witness another viewing platform of the old city. Sometimes concerts were held there and I went with some other members of staff to enjoy a light classical concert one evening.

Another place that I discovered in the Christian Quarter was the German St John, Johanniter Hostel. I knocked on the door one day and the manager gave me a tour around the building; it can accommodate twelve visitors to stay and is cheap accommodation in the old city. I was also privileged to visit the Church of the Holy Sepulchre many times, which gets very crowded. Once, I took a young lady who was in training to become a paramedic who was at the hospital for two weeks' experience. I explained that I could show her the old city, but she didn't take my advice to dress modestly. When we were approaching the entrance to the Church of the Holy Sepulchre, one of the monks who guard the church shouted to her, "You cannot come in here dressed like that," so I took her to other parts of the city and we returned another day, lesson learned.

The Church of the Holy Sepulchre contains many other chapels and side rooms administered by various Christian denominations. One secret chapel shown to me was up some steps at the side of the main Basilica and was called the Chapel of St Helena. In the 4th century when the Roman Emperor Constantine converted to Christianity his mother, Queen Helena, took a contingent of followers to the Holy Land. She wanted to visit many holy sites, maybe as one of the first people to go on a pilgrimage. She used her wealth to have churches built over the sites where the local people said the important events had taken place. (Over hundreds of years many churches have been built over each other in the Holy Land where the earth levels have altered.) The chapel is quiet and dark and ideal for meditation away from the noise in the main building. Unusually, through the chapel are steps leading down to an ancient city cistern (reservoir) that still holds water and can be viewed. Outside the chapel, the monks' cells can be seen where they live to protect the holy site.

One Sunday I attended a service in the Lutheran Church of St John. This is near the Muristan area where the first hostel for pilgrims was built at the time of the Crusades. The church has a beautiful stained-glass window dedicated to St John the Baptist, and I was pleased to hear that this church ran a day centre for poor elderly Arabs in the city, three days per week. They were encouraged to pursue art and craftwork, play board games and they were given lunch. The Order of St John still owned some buildings along the Muristan and there was a memorial garden built to inform visitors of the early St John Hospice which stood there. In 2016 the Order opened a clinic on the site of the original 12th century St John Hospice, where it treats over 5,000 walk-in patients annually. The hot dusty atmosphere tends to give rise to many eye problems. It also includes a peace garden, café, tree of hope and a museum, all open to patients, visitors and tourists.

For many weeks I tried to find the very old Crusader Church of St John in the Old City market place. I was able to walk around the outside noting the Apse (dome), but couldn't find an entrance. I asked some local people running stalls along the street and was informed that it was only opened for services at 6.00 am on Sunday mornings and some Tuesday afternoons. I set out one Tuesday afternoon and was lucky. In a small gap between two stalls was an open gate where I climbed over the surround and into a courtyard. Opposite was the small door leading into the church. The original 5th century sanctuary lies more than seven metres below street level and above it lies Byzantine ruins from the 11th to 12th century. During the 12th century the Knights of St John adopted it as their church and it was renovated. Today, it belongs to the Greek Orthodox Church who had it thoroughly repaired in the 19th century. Inside were some green and gold icons, and the artwork on the walls and ceiling was stunning; my perseverance to find it had paid off.

Another church that only opened to visitors on Tuesday afternoons was the Russian Church of St Mary Magdalene, on

Crusader Church of St John in the Old City, Jerusalem

The Russian Church

the Mount of Olives. It was managed by Russian nuns. This church was built in 1888 by Czar Alexander III and has unusual pointed golden domes typical of Muscovite church styles that can be seen from a distance. It commemorates Mary's tears as she sees Jesus on the cross. In the crypt is the Tomb of Princess Alice of Greece (Prince Philip's mother).

At the top of the hill on the Mount of Olives is the area known as Bethphage (meaning house of figs). I walked down this hill many times remembering where Jesus rode into Jerusalem on an ass. The Palm Sunday procession goes through St Stephen's Gate and ends at the Crusader Church of St Anne's.

Another of my memories from the Old City is when exiting St Anne's Crusader Church a woman suddenly appeared, shouting, "Val, Val, Hello!" She had recognised me from Aylesbury and was on a Catholic pilgrimage; I had visited her neighbour who was one of my patients. We had a little chat before her guide whisked her along to the next place to visit. This happened to me twice more. I was on holiday in Crete and a chap that I recognised from school was staying in the same hotel, along with his brother and mother. They lived above Gilroy's shop along Bletchley Road opposite the child clinic where my St John experiences started. We all spent an evening together reminiscing. Another time I was with John in Auckland, New Zealand, staying with my St John pal, Penny Blackman. Whilst having a snack in a local café, we got chatting to the waitress and found out she had emigrated to New Zealand from Aylesbury. It's a small world!

The Jaffa Gate area of the Old City is another place worth exploring. It was here that I found a chemist shop tucked away in a side street and was able to purchase some babies' bottles and sterilising tablets for a small baby being treated by Sister Meg. The father had brought the child for treatment, but the mother hadn't been able to come to the hospital because she had other children to look after and it was very difficult to get passes from the Israelis to travel. The equipment worked a treat and Sister Meg was also able to give some clothes from her store to help the family.

I went to a service at Christchurch, situated by the Jaffa Gate, but became slightly worried when I witnessed people taking drinks into the service. The service lasted for two hours and was quite evangelical in nature, unlike St George's which is more traditional. Christchurch looks on its mission to evangelise the Jews to Christianity and has a small museum documenting its history. It is opposite St David's Tower at the Jaffa Gate. This important landmark is where General Allenby and Lawrence of Arabia paraded when they entered the city in 1917 during the First World War.

On leaving St John Eye Hospital to walk down the hill in East Jerusalem I first walked past some of the foreign consulates, e.g. the Turkish and Italian ones as their Embassies are in Tel Aviv. Even walking along the road, I would meet United Nations officers, African chiefs, Arabs, and a mixture of nuns and priests. I have seen staff from World Vision, Red Cross and the UN Relief Agency around the city. Next, I would pass the Ambassador Hotel where I would go to book a taxi if I wanted to visit Israeli West Jerusalem. Jewish taxi drivers did not like to proceed up the hill to the hospital. If I wanted a taxi to go to somewhere in East Jerusalem the hospital reception would phone for one. A tram line has been built all along the main roads so it is probably much easier now to travel across the city.

Further down the hill I would reach the Anglican Cathedral Church of St George the Martyr, East Jerusalem. I would worship here on Sundays at 11.00 am. There was an earlier service but it was in Arabic, so the later English one was suitable. Sometimes I was asked to deliver the Bible reading. The church has a very good organ and excellent recitals were held. It has a side chapel dedicated to the Order of St John and a baptism pool used very rarely. Afterwards coffee would be served in the foyer giving me a chance to speak to any pilgrims who were on escorted tours. This would swell the numbers, as the congregation was not very big. The Christian numbers in the Holy Land are declining as there is constant friction between the Jews and Muslims. The Bishop of Jerusalem, Riah Abu El-Assal, who grew up in Nazareth, gave a very good presentation on Christians being caught in between, saying that his son and one of his daughters had emigrated to Canada in order to progress with their careers. The Diocese includes Jordan, Lebanon and Syria. A Confirmation Service was held whilst I was there when two teenage girls were confirmed and afterwards the Dean kindly invited the regulars to his flat for a cooked breakfast, as he was shortly to return to America. St George's has a hostel for visitors to stay, so one doesn't need to stay in expensive hotels, as hostels carry on the tradition of providing accommodation to pilgrims visiting Jerusalem.

Another favourite place near the cathedral is the American Colony Hotel. This is one of the leading hotels in the world and many famous people have stayed there, including Winston Churchill, Lawrence of Arabia, Noel Coward, as well as film stars, diplomats and world leaders. It was so relaxing to sit in the courtyard and enjoy a coffee. Some of the evenings I could have a drink in the bar and be a fly on the wall to see if I could spot anyone famous, like Jeremy Bowen from the BBC. The staff recognised me as I attended a Christmas dinner there with the hospital staff and also picked up a coach for some day trips from the reception.

This hotel has close links with the St John Eye Hospital. Its story starts when a group of pious Christians, the extended Spafford family, emigrated from Chicago in 1881. They started a new life in this large ex-pasha's mansion. On Christmas Eve, 1925, a poor Arab came to the door and explained that his wife was dying and could they look after his baby. Bertha Spafford Vester took the child in and this led to her helping other orphans and sick children. The Spafford Baby Home was founded. During the First World War the family stayed impartial and gave a lot of service to the desperate local population. Their charitable work eventually led to the building of the Spafford Children's Centre, which supports the sick and disabled children of East Jerusalem. Mothers bring their children for immunisations, some disturbed children receive psychological care and many children from disadvantaged families receive support. It is a much-needed children's centre, situated just inside the Damascus Gate. One day I had the opportunity to visit the centre and be shown around the different specialities by the Medical Director, Dr Dajani-Wielaard. At the end of the visit, she took me to the top of the building, so I could witness the panoramic view of the Old City.

On one corridor of the hotel was a small display of the work during the 20th century. During the 1960s Mrs Vester and her husband Horatio (the grandson of the colony's founder) left London and turned the building into a first-class hotel. Peter Ustinov, a family friend, planted two huge palm trees in the courtyard when the hotel was modernised. Many nationalities feel at home in the hotel and enjoy the pool, gym and beautiful bedrooms. It also has a marvellous bookshop where I found interesting and unusual books about Jerusalem, the Middle East and Lawrence of Arabia.

Mrs Vester DStJ still resided at the hotel and was a big supporter of the St John Eye Hospital since being a private patient when she had a cataract removed. I was privileged to look after her and ensure that she had everything she required. Later, when I mentioned to the hotel staff what a privilege to have Mrs Vester at the hospital, they offered me an executive room for the night at a reduced price. So, one Tuesday afternoon I settled into a lovely, large bedroom. The bed was six-foot wide and the television screen almost as big. I was given complimentary fruit, wine and newspapers. The room had two bathrooms. One had a washbasin, toilet and walk-in shower – the other had a large bath and two washbasins. I thoroughly enjoyed my bed and breakfast, apart from the Minaret next-door calling people to prayer at 5.00 am! Mrs Vester died at the hotel in 2008 at the age of 96. She requested a simple burial service at the Colony's private cemetery on Mt Scopus.

Further down the road I would reach the gate to the Garden Tomb. This is a beautiful garden, full of shrubs and flowers for pilgrims to meditate, pray and observe what a first century tomb would be like. Groups of tourists are shown around and given a presentation about early wells, a wine press and ancient ossuaries (where bones were stored). I chatted to the volunteers serving in the shop, who said if I ever wanted to return, I could volunteer to work there for six months and accommodation would be provided!

Near the Damascus Gate, where the road to Damascus used to start, there is a hall used by the Palestinians for parties and weddings called 'Dream Hall.' Sister Ann invited me to her son's wedding reception there. The staff explained that the couple had already had a civil ceremony and honeymoon but this was the family party and reception. The bride rode along the path on a horse and fireworks were let off each side of the path. When inside, the bride and groom sat on a small elevated platform and friends would go up to the bride and pin notes of money on her dress. Music and dancing followed, with the men dancing in groups and the women dancing together. There was much joking and laughing. We then sat around large tables to enjoy an Arabic buffet. Falafel and chickpeas were popular with tuna, hardboiled egg and cheese dishes. There was no alcohol, mostly Coca Cola, squashes, mint tea and coffee.

CHAPTER 21

EAST JERUSALEM, THE WEST BANK
AND THE OUTREACH TEAM

Roughly once a fortnight I was able to go with the Outreach Team into the West Bank to witness the preventative work and check-ups in the rural communities. The office photocopied my passport and was able to add me to the list travelling in the minibus. The team would load up at 7.15 am and we would pile into the vehicle. It always reminded me of the blood donor sessions back home, to unpack the equipment, set up and pack away later. It was my job to help with the unpacking, taking the fragile equipment out very carefully and make the staff cups of mint tea whenever possible. I would also take boxes of chocolates to give out to the patients patiently waiting to be seen.

The first visit was to a village near Jenine, approximately 80 miles north of Jerusalem. The team consisted of two doctors, three nurses, a health education nurse and the driver. On the journey we drove through two checkpoints where we showed our passports and IDs. A few miles from the village we stopped and enjoyed our picnic breakfast under some olive trees. (Some of the staff had been travelling since 6.00 am in order to arrive at the hospital for 7 o'clock.) Our minibus was given by The Johanniter (German St John) who obtained funds from the European Commission on behalf of St John. The clinic was held in a Community Centre that had been recently built by the Canadian Government for the Palestinians.

The team quickly set up in three rooms – the main hall was used as the waiting room and to take the patients details. The health educator would discuss problems and give out leaflets on the care of eyes. A small middle room was used by the two doctors for eye examinations and the nurse administering the eye drops. The third room was used by a nurse to conduct vision tests. Over the four hours people kept pouring into the hall – children with squints and congenital cataracts, elderly people with glaucoma (pressure at the back of the eye) and macular degeneration (age degeneration of the eye). Some people had foreign bodies removed from the eye and one boy aged 8 presented with scarring to his back and hands from a bomb explosion some time ago. He was instructed to go to a special children's clinic at Jenin Hospital. A very small gentleman showed me where the glass cups for the tea were kept and a community worker kept count of the numbers. Seventy-five people were screened, some were reassessed, others were given follow-up appointments and some were given creams and drops etc. Several people were given operation dates for the hospital in Jerusalem. It was the same procedure for going home after a tiring and busy day. Everything was packed away neatly and the locals gave us some snacks for another picnic.

The St John Outreach Programme is serving a population of 2.5 million people for ophthalmic care. It treats patients regardless of ethnicity, religion or ability to pay and was an eye opener for me! The opening of the clinics in Hebron in the south and Anabta in the north have relieved some of the outreach work, but there are so many rural communities that require assessments and health education that they need to visit five destinations per week to cover the areas.

The Palestinian people were very hospitable and would arrange for lots of mint tea and squash to be available at the hall or centre. After the clinic had finished, we were often invited to a local property for a sit-down meal or picnic. I witnessed meat being cooked in a land fill oven in the ground and sat one day in an orange grove for a meal.

Another outreach visit was to Jericho. This time we had our picnic on a hill overlooking the town. The hospital kitchen provided some food and the staff top this up. I took some hard-boiled eggs and a tin of tuna to help out! At this clinic the staff took an hour's lunch break. The senior nurse asked me if I would like to have a walk around Jericho as she had some shopping to do. We visited some Arabic shops and bought some of the lovely fresh fruit which was on display. We turned a corner and arrived at the town square where a camel auction was taking place. I was able to watch and take some photographs. A few donkeys and horses were also for sale. On another corner was Zacchaeus's tree. This is the site where Zacchaeus the tax collector was told by Jesus to come down from the sycamore fig tree as Jesus wanted to go to his house. (Luke 19 v 1) Also, this spot marks where Jesus is said to have healed the blind man. (Matthew 20 v 29)

Outreach picnic in Jericho

One day I went with the staff to the Palestinian city of Ramallah. I was shown Yasser Arafat's Mausoleum that is guarded proudly by soldiers in smart uniforms. We met up with some other health workers as it was World Diabetic Day. The idea was to parade along the main streets, encouraging people to follow us to a local hall. Here they could have free health checks to see if they had diabetes. The incidence of Diabetes amongst the Palestinian community is very high, at 12-15 percent of the population where access to health care is very limited. This figure is three times higher than in the West. Diabetic Retinopathy affects up to 80 percent of all people who have had Diabetes for ten years or more, so it was important that people were checked. In the hall there was a stall on healthy eating, care of the feet, blood sugar and blood pressure checks, plus our table for eye checks. It has the support of the World Diabetes Foundation. It was very worthwhile, but a hot tiring day.

Near the Damascus Gate in East Jerusalem is the Rockefeller Museum. This was built in 1927 with money provided by the American philanthropist, John D Rockefeller. I thought this museum was more interesting than some in West Jerusalem as it contained many artifacts from excavations in the desert and pieces from Iraq, Iran and Syria. It contains a fascinating reconstruction of a 7th century Ommayad palace and baths.

Walking away from the Eye Hospital, further up the hill I came to Mt Scopus. On this hill is a huge cemetery with many graves from the First World War. I attended the Remembrance Ceremony there on the nearest Saturday to 11th November, when hospital staff wore their formal uniforms and regalia. Matron was in a bright red dress and the other senior staff had the official cloaks with the St John Cross embroidered on the side. I wore my black officer's dress, hat and gloves. Many dignitaries were present, including consulate staff, expats, charity workers and UN officials wearing the blue beret. Representatives from the Allied Forces of the Second World

War laid wreaths. The British Consul General, Dr John Jenkins, welcomed the gathering and the Dean of St George's, Rev John Tidy, led the prayers. A Scottish piper carried out the lament.

After the ceremony, Matron led us to the grave of an Australian nurse who was killed towards the end of the war. She is the only female in the cemetery and the hospital have adopted the grave to look after. Matron explained that she had managed to contact the nurse's relatives in Australia and they were very happy for the hospital to remember her. Matron said that any visitors were invited to lay a posy on the grave, so I was asked to place the posy by the headstone, quite an honour.

Laying a posy at the Australian Nurse's Grave

Afterwards hospital transport took us to the British Consulate building where the consulate staff hosted a buffet lunch. The UK Consul General in Jerusalem has traditionally served on the St John Eye Hospital's Board of Trustees. We sat under a huge vine for some shade. This beautiful garden was full of lavender, roses and other English flowers. Home from home.

One evening I attended a concert held in the hall at the Augusta Victoria Hospital. Built in 1910, it was previously the residence of the British Governor General from the end of World War I until 1927; its square pointed tower is quite a Jerusalem landmark. Taking part in this concert were two young men playing a piano duet – one was Jewish the other a Palestinian, and they played brilliantly. There are six charity hospitals situated in East Jerusalem, including our Eye Hospital and the French St Joseph's, next-door. St Joseph's was built in 1957 and has 70 beds. This serves as a small general hospital. If any of the Eye Hospital patients require blood tests or X-rays, they could be carried out next-door. There is also a cancer hospital and a children's hospital in the area.

Nearby, at the Seven Arches Hotel, I enjoyed having a drink at sunset to observe the view across to the Old City. As it got dark and the lights gradually came on, looking across the Kidron Valley I could see hundreds of Jewish graves. Jews, if possible, like to be buried there – perhaps two of the most famous are Oskar Schindler, who rescued many Jews during the Second World War, and Robert Maxwell who became notorious for plundering many people's pensions!

One Saturday a theatre porter offered to take me to his home at Bethany. He was on duty until 2.00 pm when we set off in a local minibus. We had to squeeze through a fence to get to St Lazarus Sanctuary, built in 1954 by the Italian architect Barluzzi, incorporating 4th, 6th and 12th century remains, but it was locked up. The chap said never mind because he could show me the hole where Lazarus was kept! He prized open a manhole cover and led me down a ladder into a large hole, which led into a cave-like grotto. He said that many people just visit the church and don't see the original hole!

The theatre porter then took me to his family's house – they were all very hospitable and served me mint tea and some biscuits, then showed me around the property. When a member of the family gets married, they just build another room, a bedsit to accommodate them. They also showed me the little garden that had a few oranges growing and a small grapevine. His wife could not have children, which made them very distressed. They said how they had spent all their savings going to various specialists to see if anything could be done to help them. The wife helped with his brother's children and at a local nursery. It was very sad for them. I was given more mint tea and a bowl of fresh fruit. The brother was a security guard at one of the consulates and was given many pound coins as tips. This money wasn't much good to him as he was not able to change it, but I was able to help. He gave me the bag of change, which amounted to £70, and I was able to get him the equivalent in Shekels as this was a lot of money for this family. Afterwards the porter took me to the bus stop and saw me onto the transport.

Matron gave permission for my husband to join me for Christmas. He could bring out medication, cards and presents. Many staff were going away for Christmas, so Ahmad said that my son Matthew could stay a couple of nights in the flat and could fly over from Cyprus. Steve James explained that the hospital gave five Christian bank holidays and five Muslim holidays to staff, in order to be fair to all.

Bethlehem

We decided to go to Bethlehem for Christmas Eve and arrived at 12.00 noon. Fortunately, the taxi was able to bring us from Jerusalem through the checkpoint to Manger Square and as there were not any holdups the Israeli guards just waved us through.

We waited patiently in the crowds and eventually a large procession of Scouts paraded through the streets playing trumpets, drums and bagpipes. Girls and boys of all age groups were represented from Cubs to Venture Scouts. Later the Greek Orthodox Patriarch arrived to be welcomed for the Christmas services, but as it was very cold we went into the Bethlehem Peace Centre for shelter and a coffee. We visited a commercial museum which showed, with moving figures, how Christmas was celebrated in Poland and some traditional displays of the Nativity.

After crossing the crowd barriers, we were able to visit the Church of the Nativity. The main church had been preserved since Queen Helena's time, as the Persian invaders of 634 AD saw carvings of the Magi (people from the east,) carved around the pillars and so did not damage this church. On the ground are mosaics from the Roman era. Going down the steps and into the cave, we saw many Greek and Armenian frescos, icons and lanterns. On one side was the metal star commemorating where Jesus was born and on the other side was a trough commemorating the manger. The church had many side chapels and interesting crypts, including the burial place of St Jerome, who translated the Bible into Latin during the 5th century. The modern Catholic Chapel of St Catherine is where the annual midnight mass is broadcast all over the world. Outside we observed the bronze sculpture of St George and the Dragon.

During the afternoon we visited a community centre where local women were selling crafts and refreshments, then we took a taxi to the Shepherds Fields Church some two miles away. A Greek Orthodox Church covers the cave that has a fine 4th century mosaic floor and earlier churches and excavations can be viewed. On returning to the town we sheltered in a fast-food café where many of the procession's youngsters had gathered for refreshments, out of the cold wind. It was definitely the place for teenagers and was called Balloons.

At 8.30 pm we joined the Anglican group from St George's Cathedral and were led into a side entrance of the Church of the Nativity. A Greek chapel is made available to hold a traditional service of carols and readings. The Anglican Bishop of Jerusalem, the Greek Orthodox Patriarch and the British Consul General attended and each did a Bible reading. The British Consul General read his in perfect Arabic! The Greek Patriarch put on special robes for the service and sang his reading. As the service progressed, some security men entered the chapel followed by the Palestinian President, Mahmoud Abbas, and two TV cameras. The service stopped to allow the President to give his Christmas peace message and then the entourage left to carry on with further visits; the service continued as if nothing unusual had happened. People were queuing by now with special tickets for the midnight mass, but as we had seen enough during the twelve hours, we returned to Jerusalem in a coach for the St George's congregation. It was a very special place that I will always remember.

John, Matthew and I spent Christmas Day at the hospital and enjoyed a Christmas lunch at the nearby Askadinion Restaurant. On 26th December we took the bus to Eliat on the Red Sea where it was much warmer with clear blue skies. During the break we were able to visit the Underwater Observatory to see many tropical fish, stingrays, sea turtles and corals; Matthew went diving with the dolphins at the dolphin reef where they also assist in therapy for the disabled, whilst we relaxed in the salt and mineral pools. Eliat's modern development began in 1956 after the Suez campaign opened up the Red Sea to shipping and it is now an impressive holiday resort. It has year-round sunshine and boasts of many water sports and a vibrant night life.

Galilee

On 29th December Matthew left us for a few days in Egypt and we took the bus to Tiberius to visit the churches around the Sea of Galilee – Bethsaida, Nazareth, Capernaum and Cana, where many of the gospel stories took place. After a boat ride on the Sea of Galilee we went to the museum that houses the old fisherman's boat. Some years ago, a fisherman's boat was found during the drought year of 1985 by the shores of the Sea of Galilee. It was examined and preserved and was dated from the latter part of the first century BC to 70 AD. At 2,000 years old it gives a good idea of the fisherman's boats at the time of Christ.

We celebrated the New Year by spending time at the leisure facilities and hot mineral springs at Hammat Gader. These were thought to be the best hot springs in the world by the Romans. Some of the hotel guests celebrated the Jewish festival of Hanukkah whilst we were there, lighting many candles and praying. This ceremony commemorates the re-dedication of the Temple. Another day we were able to witness some baptisms in the River Jordan nearby. On January 3rd John flew back to the UK and I started more work in the operating theatres.

Acre

Before I left my placement, I wanted to visit Acre on the coast, as it had so much Crusader history. I was able to go on a day trip first to Caesarea then onto Acre. Caesarea was constructed by Herod in 20 BC and has a vast harbour. It has been excavated to show the remains of the city wall, a hippodrome, Roman Amphitheatre, corda (main street), fountains, Crusader tower, marble statues and mosaics. Moving on to Acre, this was the last stronghold of the Knights of St John in the Holy Land before they fled to Cyprus. The wondrously preserved subterranean complex has had the crypt, dining halls and hospice excavated and they are still finding artifacts. It had a secret underground tunnel to the harbour which enabled the Knights to flee during a siege. The Citadel built on Crusader ruins was used as a prison, and when the authorities were thwarting escapes they came across some of the buried Crusader buildings.

CHAPTER 22
WEST JERUSALEM AND ITS ENVIRONS

After Friday prayers, the staff would try to finish work early in the afternoon. I would race along the road to purchase a copy of the Jerusalem Post to find out what concerts, films and exhibitions were on in West Jerusalem the following week. West Jerusalem was very built up and reminded me of a town in America. Many Israelis speak English as their second language, so it was quite easy to explore the exciting places. One of the first places that I visited was the Biblical Zoo, where they tried to show all the animals mentioned in the Old Testament. I spent a pleasant Sunday afternoon walking around a lake and particularly remember the black swans. A café was a welcome retreat for lunch that day. On another occasion I visited a natural history museum set in an old Arabic house.

One Friday I went to Tico House. This was an ex-doctor's house who came from Moravia in 1912 after completing his studies in Vienna. His wife was an artist and began drawing the landscapes around Jerusalem. After their deaths it became a centre for exhibitions, art displays, concerts and cultural events. Concerts were held regularly on Fridays and I enjoyed several visits there. The complex had a restaurant and display telling of the house's history and many retired Israelis enjoyed meeting their friends there for a meal. I always carried a copy of my passport in case anyone required information about me. Security could be very tight at times and searches were common.

Nearby I found an artist's gallery. His paintings were of his vision of the new Jerusalem and his ideas of the psalms and the second coming of the Messiah. I purchased some large postcards of his beautiful pictures and used them to illustrate some of my talks. I also visited the Israeli Museum, which was opened in 1965. Among the gems are a 17th century Italian Synagogue and another from Cochin, India. It also has the Shrine of the Book which contains the Dead Sea Scrolls in a special gallery that can be lowered into a vault, should an air raid or earthquake occur. In another area I viewed the model of Jerusalem as it was at the time of Christ before AD 70 and the destruction of Jerusalem and the Temple Mount.

An important museum is the Yad Vashem, a memorial to the six million Jews who perished in the European Holocaust of the Second World War. It is a modern museum with paths connecting each gallery. There are thousands of photographs showing Jewish families who lost their lives in the concentration camps and piles of shoes, dentures and belongings taken from them as prisoners. It is a very moving and sobering place to visit, showing man's inhumanity to man.

The Bible Lands Museum, although modern, was not so interesting for me. It didn't seem to have the character and atmosphere of the other museums. It contained a theatre and on the last Friday of the month held a cheese and wine evening in the foyer, from where one could proceed into the theatre for a concert. I enjoyed a Simon and Garfunkel evening, a Gilbert and Sullivan concert and a 1960s pop evening, to name but a few. Central Jerusalem has a large shopping mall, again where bags are searched as you enter and leave, but I enjoyed shopping there as it had a bookshop that sold English paperbacks. I would have lunch, then see a film in the multiplex cinema. Another place that I discovered was Jerusalem Sherover Theatre complex. This housed a concert hall, theatre, cinema, bookstall and restaurant. There were lots of places to keep me amused when off duty, but sadly they were not available to the Palestinians who I was working with.

The main bus station had high security and I ventured there one Saturday to go on a visit to Ein Karim, a little village in the hill country just outside Jerusalem where John the Baptist grew up. (Luke 1 v 65) It is in a very pretty valley and has a church on each bank. One church represents where John was born and the other the place where he lived. Further along the road is Mary's well, said to be the place where Virgin Mary met Elizabeth when awaiting the birth of their babies. On the way back I ventured into the large Hadassah Hebrew University Medical Centre. The hospital has 2,000 beds and also contains a hotel and shops. I visited the synagogue there as it contains the famous Jewish artist Marc Chagall's stained-glass windows to view and admire. They represent the sons of the Patriarch Jacob from whom descended the twelve tribes of Israel.

Bethlehem

Another Saturday morning, I ventured on my own to Bethlehem. The taxi could only take me to the separation wall where I showed my passport and eventually was able to go to the other side. At the passport control I saw Lena, one of the hospital cleaners, who was trying to go through. She asked if I was OK and I replied yes. I didn't have the hassle that she experienced trying to travel. I then took another taxi to Manger Square. Around the square are several souvenir shops that sell the lovely olive wood nativity sets. I had already purchased one that was hand carved, but now many are made in a factory by machine. One of the nurse's husbands ran a shop there. Another place nearby was an Arabic museum. This was run by a women's co-operative rights group and highlighted life of years gone by. It displayed an old house and farming tools. In the basement was an area where the people would keep a goat or cow for milk and also chickens. Sometimes they had a horse or donkey. I purchased a table runner, hand made in traditional Arabic design.

The square also held the Peace Centre showing various displays of the area. Along a lane to the side of the Church of the Nativity I found the Church of the Milk Grotto commemorating Mary's milk and the feeding and care of Jesus by his mother. Underneath the Franciscan Chapel is a cave where it is said the Holy Family sheltered before fleeing to Egypt. To the other side of the square was a community hall, where a women's group were serving soup and hot drinks to visitors and tourists.

On another visit to Bethlehem I visited the Bible Lands building where the charity looks after poor, disadvantaged or disabled children. St John provides eye care for them and help from the Children's Spectacle Fund. They have several centres around the Middle East and are funded by the Bible Lands Society based at High Wycombe that produce the Bethlehem Carol Sheet at Christmas.

On another occasion, I accompanied some hospital staff to visit the Holy Family Maternity Hospital in Bethlehem. This is run by the Catholic Sovereign Military Order of Malta. Originally founded by the French Daughters of Charity in 1888, it was completely refurbished in 1990 by the Sovereign Order. More than 2,500 babies are delivered here each year and the Eye Hospital arranges visits to check the eyes of the mothers and new-borns, and it also holds follow-up clinics. I viewed the special care baby unit, the education centre, the chapel and the clinics.

My first day trip from Jerusalem was a coach trip to the Dead Sea. This is the lowest place on earth, some 1,290 feet below sea level. Measuring 48 miles in length and 11 miles across, it contains high solid contents of salts, magnesium, sodium, calcium, potassium chlorides and magnesium bromide. In recent decades the water-line has retreated with exploitation for industrial and agricultural purposes by both Israel and Jordan. On the way we passed Bedouin camps that had lots of goats wandering about. I witnessed a shepherd boy tending the goats with a Walkman tape machine to relieve the boredom. The Bedouins now have piped water so don't move around much. They also want their children to get some schooling.

As soon as we left Jerusalem, we were in the Judean desert. We drove past the Inn of the Good Samaritan – ruins of a Byzantine Monastery of St Joachim mark the spot close to the highway. The guide pointed to a cave where the Dead Sea Scrolls were found by two shepherd boys in 1947. The scrolls were in seven earthenware jars and contained priceless biblical manuscripts. Some of the coach party continued on to visit Masada, the Zealots' rocky fortress, but seven of us were dropped off at the spa by the Dead Sea.

The first thing we did was to change into our swimsuits and visit the hot sulphur baths for fifteen minutes. The waters are full of minerals that are good for the skin. After a shower, I went outside for a swim in the lovely pool, then took the land train to the water's edge, to paddle and float in the Dead Sea. The Israelis and Jordanians have used a lot of the salt water, so the sea has receded over 1,000 metres. There were large stones and pillars of salt all around and several taps of fresh water in case anyone accidently gets any salt water in the mouth or eyes. Every so often fighter jets from the Israeli Air Force would fly overhead to guard the border with Jordan. After another shower I took the land train to the mud area and covered my face, arms and legs with mud and allowed it to dry in the warm sunshine. This is the original beauty mudpack! The next process is to have a sulphur shower to wash off the mud and soak in another sulphur pool before going to lunch in the cafeteria. After lunch we went to sunbathe around the swimming pool. On the way back to Jerusalem, we visited the factory and shop where all the beauty products of the Dead Sea are manufactured and sent all over the world.

Another evening I was able to join a group to explore the Jewish Western Wall's tunnels that run alongside the thick walls of the

Temple Mount. Excavations have uncovered remains dating from the time of King Solomon. They are only open at certain times with a guide. We first were taken up some steps to view the old city over some traditional Jewish dwellings, then down some steps where the guide managed to switch some lights on for us to view the passageway. We toured the ancient Herodian street at a depth of 50 feet below ground. When we reached a central point, we were shown some excavations and artifacts that had been recovered, then he led us further along the tunnels to where we were under some Palestinian houses and could hear the families speaking above. The group asked lots of questions, some of which were in English and some in Hebrew; this was quite an unusual evening that tourists would not know about or be able to attend.

Jericho

I had some more adventures travelling to Jericho on my own. I was given some days off for the Muslim feast of Eid. The first night I was the only resident in the hotel and the manager put me in one of their chalets by the pool. The chef cooked a dinner just for me! On the second night many Palestinian families came and I was moved to a hotel room. I so wanted to explore Jericho, the city of palms, famous for growing dates, bananas and oranges; the oldest city on earth with settlements dating back 9,000 years.

On my first day I went by cable car to the Mount of Temptation where there is a marvellous view of Jericho, the Dead Sea and the Allenby Bridge crossing to Jordan. I walked along the ridge to the Mount of Temptation Greek Monastery. Along with some Russian pilgrims, the monks showed me a very old rock where they commemorated Jesus in the wilderness, fasting for 40 days and driving away the devil; also, to be seen at Jericho were excavations of Herod's three palaces from AD35. I visited the Hisham's Palace ruins of AD 743. This was the elaborate winter resort of the tenth Ummayad Caliph Walid I of Damascus. It has a pillared courtyard, with the remains of two mosques, heated bathing rooms and well-preserved mosaic floors. On another site a 7th century Synagogue floor has been excavated along with the remains of an aqueduct that carried water to the city.

Jericho was a hive of activity. A baker was rolling out dough and putting it in a little oven that was placed on a cart in one of the town's squares. The barber's shop had a queue and vegetable sellers were shouting their prices. The electrical shops were filled with oil filled radiators and every so often someone went by leading a donkey loaded with produce. Children were having rides on ponies and donkeys.

The next day I took a taxi to the Wadi Kelt area to visit St George's Monastery, which is situated in the Valley of the Shadow of Death (Psalm 23), a grim valley with birds squawking. The monks have placed large crosses on the surrounding hills to protect pilgrims. This monastery was built in 1901 and originally had twelve monks living there, but now has only three left. They showed me a glass coffin with the embalmed body of John the Hermit, a recluse Romanian monk found dead at the foot of the valley in 1960. The monks loved the holy man so much that they decided to embalm him and keep him with them. The monks were hospitable and gave me a drink and let me rest. Then they took me to Elijah's cave above the monastery where Elijah found safety and shelter and was said to have lived and been fed by ravens. Two lads with donkeys wanted to give me a ride back up the hill in order to earn some money and take me to the awaiting taxi, but I declined and graciously let two elderly ladies have a ride so that I could take my time walking up the hill away from the steep ledges!

The next day it was time to leave Jericho and head to the spa resort and Kibbutz at Ein Gedi. However, the Palestinian taxi driver would only take me to the Dead Sea Highway in Jerusalem because the area was Israeli. He left me at a bus stop and said that a regular service operated and I would see a bus shortly. I hoped that I wouldn't be stranded in the Judean desert! Thankfully, about twenty minutes later a bus came along and took me to Ein Gedi.

I had a booking at the spa hotel and joined tourists to enjoy the hot sulphur springs, pools and mud baths. The spa is run by a Kibbutz which was celebrating its 55th anniversary and took tourists from all around the world. The area has ancient underground lakes whose waters passed through rocks causing chemical changes. On the way to the surface the waters mix with the waters of the Dead Sea resulting in a special composition of which the most important element is sulphur, so people from all over the world visit the spa to help their psoriasis, arthritis, rheumatism and other bone and muscle ailments.

The next day a guide led all the guests to see the amazing botanical garden and cacti display; he then took us up a hill to the nature reserve. The hillside has fresh water springs that drain down from the Hebron Hills. We observed a lovely 300ft high waterfall and saw some goats and mountain rabbits that the guide said were related genetically to the elephant. We saw many types of birds and semi-tropical vegetation. The Kibbutz had an impressive sports hall and swimming pool; the restaurant food was cosmopolitan to suit all tastes and during the evening we watched some Israeli folk dancing. The next day I took a taxi to the hospital and went back to work.

Tel Aviv

On a weekend in March, I was able to travel on the light railway to Tel Aviv, the commercial centre and hub of cultural life of Israel. It's hard to imagine that less than one hundred years ago the area was only sand dunes. The railway track winds along the valleys and I was able to see the pretty, wild, spring flowers that grow naturally on the banks. There were anemones, cyclamen and poppies. When I checked into the beach-front hotel, I was given an upgrade because it was the quiet season with very few tourists. I appreciated the complimentary bowl of fruit and bottle of wine! I visited the large Diaspora Museum dedicated to the history of the Jews in different countries and their festivals and traditions. It records the spreading of Jews around the world. On the Sunday I spent the day relaxing in Jaffa, which translated means 'beautiful port'. It can trace its history back 3,500 years. Today it is famous for its Artists' Quarters and Jaffa oranges.

CHAPTER 23
KEEP ME TRAVELLING ALONG THE ROAD

Petra Jordan

During my stay in Jerusalem, I became friendly with Jane and Peter Tapley. Jane was an orthoptist and had volunteered to work in the orthoptist children's clinic for a year. Peter was a retired teacher and came to help at a Palestinian girls' school near the hospital. They were given a comfortable top floor flat above me and invited me around for drinks. They were planning to have a long weekend to travel to Petra, the beautiful rose-coloured city in Jordan, which became a UNESCO World Heritage Site in 1985. Peter hired a car and we travelled along the Judean Desert to the Allenby Bridge and crossed into Jordan. We travelled south to the port of Aquaba and spent the night there. It's a busy Arabic town with a large Jordanian flag flying in the harbour. The next day we drove along the Wadi Rum (where Lawrence of Arabia had his adventures) and reached our hotel in Petra.

Early the next morning we walked into the excavated Petra. At the entrance on the left-hand side was the Queen Noor Welfare Centre which stables the animals that give rides to the tourists. On producing our passports and paying 51 dinars, we walked through the red sandstone gorge known as 'the siq' with walls 70 metres high and 1.2 kms long that had different coloured strata running through the rocks. Many of the rocks had been painted years ago. Petra is the feminine name for Peter, meaning rock or stone. In front of us was the Treasury where historians think that treasure was stored by the Nabataean traders. The city became rich between 400BC- 106AD, as it was on a main trading route between the Red Sea and the Mediterranean. The Nabataeans built an impressive conduit water system with dams and cisterns. They were ancient Arabic nomadic tribes and copied Greek, Roman and Egyptian ideas in their buildings, including the Great Temple, the Winged Lion Temple and the carvings on many tombs.

This huge city comprised 102 square miles and was built to illuminate the red rock by the sun for their sacred worship. As we walked along, Bedouin children approached us to purchase souvenirs; they still live nearby and some occupy the many caves. Along the route are the remains of the Roman colonnade street, a theatre, an ancient synagogue and some pretty mosaic floors from a Byzantine church that was discovered in 1990. After passing the huge plain, we climbed up the 840-step path to the 2nd century monastery. The city was mostly abandoned after a shift in trade during Roman times and suffered two earthquakes, but the 6th-8th century Byzantine Church proves that other groups used the area, including the Crusader Franks in the 14th century. Opposite was a refreshment tent, which was very welcome. Peter and Jane, being avid walkers, wanted to continue another two or three miles, but as we had reached the edge of the city I decided to slowly walk back to have another look at the spectacular ruins. By this time, it was getting very busy and many tourists were riding along on camels, donkeys, horses and carts. It was a beautiful experience to explore the lovely city that was buried under the sand until the Swiss explorer John Lewis Burkhardt rediscovered it in 1812. (He bequeathed his papers to Cambridge University.)

Back near the hotel I found an authentic Hamman (a Turkish bath and massage room) where I experienced the steam room, the washing with soap and water, then the scrub, followed by a massage on a marble bed. It was quite roughly given by two Arabic ladies, but I felt wonderful afterwards with the aches and pains of the walk banished. The next day we travelled back, following one of my best adventures!

Cyprus

Whilst I was in Jerusalem, Matthew was working at Foleys School in Cyprus. I had visited him halfway through my stay at the hospital because the three-month Israeli visa required renewing, so I had a fair idea of the set up in Limassol. I managed to gain a placement with the Cyprus Cancer Nurses Association based in Limassol. It was formed over thirty years ago to give palliative care to patients in their own homes and provide support to the carers. It is the only home-based nursing service, as they don't have any district nurses in Cyprus. Many Sri Lankan and Filipino girls are employed by families to look after elderly people and the disabled. There were 15 cancer nurses, mostly British nurses married to Cypriots; five in Paphos, five in Larnaca and five in Limassol. I gave two workshops to the nurses, on infection control, health and safety and anaphylaxis. Some student nurses from Nicosia Hospital attended the second day.

I spent another two days with Jo, Jennine and Yolande experiencing home visits. I watched them perform wound care and set up a syringe driver to give slow doses of sedatives and pain relief. On one visit a nurse took out a pressure mattress, cot sides and a commode. On another visit, one of the Sri Lankan carers took the nurse aside and explained that the relatives had kept her passport and she wasn't getting her day off a week. This made the nurse angry; it was my first encounter of modern-day slavery! The nurse phoned the relative and demanded that the carer be given her passport back and insisted that the girl must have one complete day away each week or the nursing service would be withdrawn. Part of the nurse's remit is to monitor medication and teach carers how to administer drugs properly; they also spent a lot of time counselling relatives and arranging doctors' visits. They are providing a much-needed community service in Cyprus to keep patients comfortable.

The summer season was in full swing and I so enjoyed two open-air concerts, one outside Limassol and the other at Larnaca. One was an evening to celebrate the 'Magic of the Musicals' and the other a concert performed by the Greek singer, Nana Mouskouri. The Holiday Inn Hotel had a new open-air pool along the seafront, and a multiplex cinema had recently opened in Limassol so there was plenty going on.

I visited the Akrotiri St John Division at the British Forces Base. Many members had moved to other bases, so a new officer had been appointed to get the division up and running again. There were twelve members, including six new ones, so the first meeting was held to discuss the programme and duties. We also went through the patient report forms. The following week I gave a two and a half hour moving and handling session. The next week we ran through equipment kept on the ambulances. I had arranged to take part in a First Aid duty with the members, but it was just after the Middle East troubles with Lebanon and Syria had started again. The duty was cancelled and the members assisted the refugees who arrived at Limassol port and were then taken to Larnaca Airport to be sent to other countries. Cyprus Island St John still hold their Investitures at the Kolossi Crusader Castle and the lovely 'Commandery of St John' (Commandaria Cypriot dessert wine native to Limassol), that is still made nearby, which I was able to sample! I stayed in Cyprus for ten weeks, all through the summer. John came out at the end of July, but felt the heat greatly – milk purchased at the supermarket turned sour before it reached my kitchen! Fortunately, I was able to take on Matthew's bungalow and hire car and at the end of the stay my dear friend Dot spent a week with me and we explored some of the island.

"Hospice is not a place; it is a concept of care."
Dame Cecily Saunders

During 2007 my son Matthew was working for St John in the International Department; he made a lot of contacts abroad and Antigua St John asked him if he would go out and run some First Aid courses so that their trainers could learn the modern methods. He wanted another trainer, and as no one wanted to go with him I volunteered as it was a fantastic opportunity to train in the Caribbean. Grace Cephas-Lewis was the Association Training Director and set up accommodation for us at the Sun Sail Colina four-star holiday resort. Their manager agreed to provide rooms and meals if we would run a four-day First Aid at Work Course for his staff. A cheap hire car was also made available for our use to explore the island. The resort was famous for its sailing and sail boat training so First Aid was very important. Another trainer from St John Jamaica was Clembert Powell, Jamaica's Training Director, who also joined us to learn the new methods. We gave training to members of the public at the Brigade's Headquarters in the middle of the island – one lady I remember was the wife of the manager of Sandals, the five-star holiday resort. We gave sessions to another hotel and to the island's civil defence army group. This enabled St John members to witness the different methods of teaching.

I was introduced to Agnes Meek, who ran the care side of St John. Agnes was an incredible lady (she has since been promoted in the Order of St John) – she set up a community palliative care service for people suffering from cancer who would be nursed at home. Her care assistants took out medical comforts, provided sitters to relieve the relatives, and supplied medication and oxygen that their doctor had prescribed. I was also able to witness the island's Rotary Club deliver meals on wheels to the elderly and poorer families, and met Alison Archer, a lady who published the island's tourist publications and wholeheartedly supported the scheme. She took us to her house and we were able to meet her mother and brother, John, who had mental health problems. I was able to give Alison some suggestions about his management, for which she was grateful, as their mental health services were basic. Alison took me to the island's small mental health hospital where she visited regularly to take books and magazines for the residents. Another experience was going with Agnes on her visits when she was able to give meal vouchers and grocery vouchers to the carers of the sick patients.

The tourists usually only see the coastal, more affluent side of the island. Inland there is much poverty and many living in substandard shacks. Agnes and her volunteers run a charity shop, which brings in much-needed cash to run the service and hoped at that time to acquire a part of the old Holberton Hospital for a Palliative Care Ward. (This she achieved in later years.)

The highlight of our stay was a meeting with the island's Governor General, Sir James Carlisle, who was the President of St John; we took tea with him and Matthew presented him with a defibrillator and banner for St John use. He gave us a signed book of the island, and said that First Aid was particularly important in 2007 as the Cricket World Cup was being held in Antigua. Another day we helped at a fundraising golf tournament to raise funds for charity and met Sir Vivian Richards, the famous Antiguan cricketer. Interestingly the expat organising the day came from Beaconsfield! It was a great fundraising day and four charities benefitted with over £5,000 each.

Agnes became a good friend and twelve months later invited me to return to Antigua to run a care course for the public and her care assistants. This was held at the Brigade's hall and again a car

Tea with the Governor General, Antigua, 2007

enabled me to see various parts of the island. This time I stayed
in Agnes's flat, which was under her split-level house near the
Cedar Valley Golf Course. Water was scarce and any water used
for my shower was collected in a bowl that I stood in and then
used to water her flowers! Agnes loved her golf and took me
around the golf course in her golf buggy to meet her friends. I
also went with her to church on Palm Sunday and joined the
procession around the outside of the church waving our palms.
Another highlight was when I went to hear the local Caribbean
church community sing, with wonderful powerful voices, their
rendition of Stainer's 'The Crucifixion.'

I was able to perform two four-day care courses and left them
teaching materials and bereavement folders. One day I
accompanied Agnes to visit a family that had just lost their 8-
year-old son to cancer. He had died at home in his mother's
arms. We gave our condolences amidst the weeping and wailing
of many friends and relatives outside the house. Many people

from the village came to the house and brought food and drink. It was like a wake outside in typical Caribbean style.

Every Sunday, barbecue evenings are held up the hill at Shirley Heights, so one Sunday I joined the crowd for dancing, food and drinks. As the sun set, I enjoyed the marvellous view of lights being lit all around Nelson's Shipyard, the area at the bottom of the hill. Another day, Agnes took me to the Island Museum which records the history of the slaves arriving on the island and people coming from other countries who have enabled the island to become prosperous. Tourism and fishing are now the main industries, as sugar and cotton growing are carried out elsewhere.

Hospice supporter, Alison Archer, arranged for me to have a beautiful day trip on a schooner sailing around the island, with drinks and a meal included. The only problem was that I took a sea sickness tablet at the start of the return journey which sent me to sleep and I missed the place to exit the boat! I got off at the next landing and took a taxi back to Cedar Valley!

St Lucia

Saga Holidays offered to place volunteers in several poor countries where teaching would help deprived areas. After writing a 500-word application stating why I wanted to help, and getting CRB checks and references, I had the privilege to spend a month in May 2013 in St Lucia helping at Morne Du Dan Government Primary School. We had first class accommodation at the Saga Bel Jou Hotel and were driven to the school each day in the hotel's minibus. Six ladies met at the airport and it was the first time I was given a room upstairs in the new Dreamliner aeroplane! Three ladies went to a school for disabled children nearby and I went with Tina and Louvaine up a long steep hill to the junior school.

Gradually we found our feet and became used to the running of the school. Tina worked well with the sports teacher and was

First Aid lesson in St Lucia

Volunteers leaving for school in St Lucia

able to get painting carried out in the playground for hopscotch and athletics. Louvaine stayed with one class and developed their reading skills, as it was World Book Week whilst we were there. I was assigned to Mr Du Boulay's class, which was the top class, and gave some music sessions to them, but was also asked to provide First Aid Training to the whole school as time went on. I took each class for three one-hour sessions so that they were able to have the three-hour basic Priorities in First Aid certificates presented at the end of our placement. I was able to borrow the Resusci-Anne from the island's St John Headquarters nearby and gave a donation.

Most of the teachers had second jobs as their pay was poor. Mr Du Boulay was a journalist for the local newspaper and another teacher was a singer at one of the tourist's restaurants. We soon discovered that some children could not afford to purchase a lunch as they only just managed the money for the school bus. We gave them our packed lunches from the hotel as we had cooked breakfasts in the all-inclusive accommodation.

Teaching resuscitation

When we returned to the hotel in the afternoon we would shower and have a swim as it was very humid and hot weather. Fruit was served on long kebab sticks around the pool and we could relax until the evening meal. I took some DVDs with me and was able to play them in my bedroom. Each evening we had marvellous Caribbean entertainment and one evening we went to Marigot Bay for a meal and had a look around the marina to inspect the expensive yachts moored there.

Our favourite place was at Pigeon Island National Park, which was near the hotel and had a lovely sandy beach. It had the remains of an old fort on the headland. It was safe for bathing and some diving was taught there. My friends, Dot and Robin, were holidaying on the island whilst I was there, so they spent a day with me at my resort and I spent a day with them at their beach resort.

The island's most famous person is Derek Walcott, a famous painter, poet and playwright who was awarded the Nobel Prize for Literature in 1992. He has a town square named after him. Also in the square is the World War II Memorial. This had the name of a Mr Du Boulay, the son of a plantation owner who had been a 22-year-old RAF pilot. The teacher's ancestors had been slaves at the plantation in an earlier era and were given their masters' surnames.

One Saturday afternoon we were entertained by watching a Caribbean wedding take place on the hotel lawns. We could watch from outside our rooms on the terrace; we enjoyed the music and partying. Another day we went to the Diamond Botanical Gardens and enjoyed the sulphur mineral baths and splendid waterfall. One day we went on a boat ride around the island, which gave us a wonderful view of the Pitons, the famous hills that rise from the beach on the southwest of the island. We also went on a day trip to the island of Martinique. This is a French island and very expensive. Most of the time was spent inspecting the wonderful tropical fruit in the covered market.

Interestingly, it has a statue in the main square to Lady Hamilton, Lord Nelson's mistress.

Our three colleagues from the school for the disabled invited us to see their school. The headmistress was very dedicated and gave talks to groups, which helped raise funds. The school made upside down rag dolls that were sold at the hotel and I still treasure the one that I purchased. Soon it was time to say goodbye to them all and we felt that the children had enjoyed our company and learned some fresh ideas. At the last assembly, the headmistress presented each of us with a large holiday bag and matching sarong. We gave our driver a bottle of rum purchased from a distillery we had visited and each child in our class was given a little toy as a keepsake. I have remained friends with Tina and Louvaine and we have met up from time to time since.

CHAPTER 24
EXPLOITS IN CAPE TOWN

"I can do all things through him who strengthens me."

Philippians 4.13

I was looking through a magazine one day when I read an article about the Exchange Experience Placements (EEPS). This was a joint venture run by the Anglican and Methodist churches to encourage people to volunteer their skills to help people in developing countries. Volunteers usually went for a six-month placement and were required to attend training at the United Church of the Ascension College in Birmingham and Selly Oak Centre for Mission Studies, linked to Birmingham University. Habib Nadir was in charge of the scheme so I wrote to him, and after all the checks and references I was booked on the course in 2007. We were a small group of around ten students of all ages and different skills from social worker, teacher, technology student, scientist to agricultural student. Some of the training included beliefs in other cultures, customs and expectations. The reverse culture effect was included for when we returned.

Cape Town

My mission was to support and teach the staff at St Anne's Mother and Baby Home in Woodstock, a suburb of Cape Town, South Africa. It was founded in 1904 by some Christian women of the province. Their vision was of St Anne helping her daughter, Mary, who was an unmarried mother. I had flight

Habib Nadar, Training Officer USPG, 2007

tickets with Namibia Airways, but was delayed at Gatwick for 24 hours and put up in the Hilton Hotel whilst the aeroplane was serviced. When I did eventually fly, we stopped at Windhoek, the capital of Namibia, and I was put up in a safari lodge for eight hours, as I had missed my connection to Cape Town.

Poor Father John Oliver, the Rector of St Mark's Church, finally met me at the airport some 36 hours later. He brought me to St Mark's Rectory flat that I would be sharing with a student and a social worker. Father John explained about District Six. It was given the name District Six in 1867 when it linked the city to the port. In 1950, under the Apartheid Government, the Group Area

Act was passed and in 1966 the Government forcibly evacuated 60,000 people living there to the Cape Flatlands, outside the main Cape Town area. Only the church and a mosque were left and the University of Cape Town buildings that wrapped around the church. Since those years, the congregation of mixed ethnicity has loyally bussed to the church on Sundays. I understood this more when I visited the District Six Museum founded in 1994 to keep the memories alive.

Father John said that I would require a car to travel about in, as I needed to be very careful about security because crime was very high in Cape Town. (At that time there were 50 people murdered in South Africa each day!) I was given three days to settle in and managed to find a car dealer that rented cars to students. I could rent a car by the month from him – this was all self-funded. I would provide my own meals and pay a nominal rent for my stay each month.

The flat was on the hillside looking towards Table Mountain and the bedroom looked out across Cape Town Bay. I was given the large guest bedroom, which had built-in cupboards and a newish bed. The main drawback was that it had wooden windows that were rotting which let in a lot of the breezes. The bathroom next-door was adequate but needed updating. The kitchen had recently been refitted but had no washing machine. If it was a mild day the wooden conservatory was very pleasant to have meals in.

Nydean, the social worker, had her own rented TV in the lounge and kindly let me watch it with her for the news and current affairs programmes, but otherwise hogged it herself as she was addicted to the soap programmes! Carol, the student, shared some food and meals with me and we explored the Natural History Museum together and a food festival at the Exhibition Centre. The rectory office was situated in the basement of the flat, and I was introduced to Rentia Van Niekirk, the parish secretary, who became my close friend and adviser during the placement.

Happy times outside St Mark's, Cape Town, with Rentia and Father John

Many of the ethnic groups had been brought to the colony as slaves and had adopted their masters' names. (The surname Van Niekirk was quite common.) Rentia invited me to her house for meals and I met her husband Tony and two grown up children. She took me into town on the regular minibus service for the estate and I purchased some flannelette sheets, a hot water bottle and a thick dressing gown. I hadn't appreciated that April to October would be their winter in the southern hemisphere, and it could be very cold at night and in the morning without any heating, although the daytime was a very pleasant sunny 18-20 degrees.

We had an African lady called Fancy who would come each week to clean the flat, as she was very poor. This was the accepted thing to help her earn money to support her grandchild. She wanted to do my washing as there was no washing machine in the flat. I gave her some washing, but she bashed the clothes so much that they were no good afterwards. I gave her some money to help with the cleaning but much preferred to clean my own room and do the laundry in the laundrette in town.

Rentia took me to The Gardens, a small shopping mall on the way into the city. I spent many hours there purchasing groceries, getting my photographs developed and enjoying reading the newspaper whilst having coffee. On Tuesday evenings we would go with Sharna, her daughter, to the cinema in the Victoria and Albert Mall at the waterfront, as it was half price and we could watch the latest films. When Tony found out about my First Aid experience, he booked me for two sessions at his church youth club. Teenagers were having sleepovers in the church hall so I had a captive audience. Tony also managed to get me a lot of First Aid equipment from his firm and I was able to make up several First Aid packs for St Anne's Home.

Tony and Rentia took me for a ride around Cape Town to get my bearings – one place was Lions Head and Signal Hill, which gives breath-taking views of the City Bowl and the Atlantic coastline. Every day at noon a cannon is fired from the battery, which was built by the British in 1890 to defend the harbour. Another favourite place was the Rhodes Monument, which was made of white granite in Doric temple style situated on the slopes of Devil's Peak. It was designed by Sir Herbert Baker as a tribute to Cecil Rhodes and unveiled in 1912 – at this spot we could enjoy a coffee and admire the views.

Whilst I was visiting, St Mark's celebrated the church's 125th birthday, and a dance was held in one of the local halls which gave me a better chance to get to know some of the congregation. Later I went with some of the parishioners on a parish weekend to Knysna. They seemed only interested in shopping, but I did manage to visit a small elephant park whilst at Knysna.

The working day at St Anne's started with devotions at 8.30 am consisting of Bible readings and testimonials. I would then see the programme for the week and discuss the training sessions with the staff. They had secretarial staff, a housekeeper, cleaners, occupational therapists, social workers and outside specialists coming in for sessions with the mothers. The aim was to enable the mothers to acquire some life skills to be independent enough to obtain jobs. Martin was in charge of the children's section as they were a handful and Blessing was in charge of the babies and nursery area. She was a big 'Mama' and sung lullabies to the babies and taught the toddlers to say their prayers and enjoy stories. She was an excellent role model for the mothers who did not have much idea of parenting.

My teaching sessions with the staff included not only First Aid, but child care, emergency child birth, the making up of baby feeds, health and safety, HIV/Aids, safeguarding and fire safety. The home had no fire safety policy and the doors were all locked, as they feared their aggressive partners could find out where the women had shelter. Health and safety was also very slack in the country and mothers were short changing the powder for feeds to make it go further. My remit broadened as time went on and I gave teaching sessions to the mothers, but this could be quite difficult as Afrikaans was their main language. A member of staff or one of the women would translate and I was able to use posters, flipcharts, and leaflets to get the message across. Some of the mothers were young girls who had become pregnant and had nowhere to go; others had been abandoned by their husbands and some had HIV/Aids and came from homes with huge social problems, but they were treated with dignity and understanding. Social workers would

Children's Playground, St Anne's Home

With Blessing in the nursery

work hard to find them suitable housing and employment after the placement, often as cleaners, security guards, shop assistants, or garage forecourt attendants.

One girl gave birth during the night at the home before an ambulance arrived and when I went in the next morning the staff told me it was providence that I had given the emergency childbirth session only the week before. Another girl had been thrown out by her parents when she became pregnant, and although only 16 she looked much older. I befriended her and took her along to the Child Welfare Clinic for the baby to be weighed, checked and given the immunisations. The incidence of HIV/Aids was very high and the mothers would need regular visits to the clinics to collect their Anti-Retroviral Drugs (ARVs). These were provided free. We were careful not to sit near any of the elderly men attending the clinic for a Tuberculosis check-up, as that was also very prevalent in South Africa.

I found the clinics and hospital spotlessly clean with black and white staff working well together. They were State run so the women did not have to pay. One baby developed pneumonia and I took the mother and baby to the Red Cross Memorial Hospital, which is a specialist children's hospital, rather like Great Ormond Street Hospital in London. They kept the baby in one night to ensure the medication was working, but the next day, with pressure on beds, the mother was given the baby back and kept it tied to her breast in the African way. This is how they looked after their babies – there were no prams, pushchairs or baby equipment.

Another project for me was to give sessions to some of the children after school as usually they were bored and played on the swings and slides in the front garden. Once a week they had drum practice in the training room, which they loved, doing all the rhythms and beats, so another day I would try and give some health sessions.

This went well for a few weeks until I did a session on flossing and caring for the teeth. They were in a particularly mischievous mood that day and the session ended in a water fight! Another day a film crew came to offer the women a free facial and make up session. It did much for the women's self-esteem and they felt very glamorous afterwards. The children loved to watch this session. A lot of filming is carried out around the coast of Cape Town as the light and climate are so good.

During the half term I took the children to the small medical museum by the waterfront. A medical intern showed them the displays and gave a talk, which fascinated Martin and the minibus driver, as they did not get a chance to visit such places. We sat on the front lawn of the museum chatting and enjoying cartons of squash, a pleasure denied these children.

Elizabeth Peterson, the director of the home, suggested other projects for me. I think that they wait to see if the volunteer is capable and reliable and if they will stay six months before giving out other ideas. One was to help with the feeding programme in the township – she took me along to visit her father who was involved in this, but it did not seem as if they needed much help.

The other suggestion was to help get a bungalow prepared for four families to live in, thus giving them a fresh start as they would have jobs in the factories nearby. The property was at Ruyterach, an industrial suburb of Cape Town. It had four bedrooms and had been given by the Council for the home to rent, on the women's behalf. It was decorated in bright colours and several bunk beds had been donated. My mission was to help equip it and make it more comfortable for the families to move in.

I purchased curtains, bedding, towels, cushions, a mirror, clock, ironing board, crockery, cutlery and kitchen utensils to give them a start. It was ideal for me to drive around and find cut-price stores. I was able to persuade Elizabeth that four families would be unhygienic and overcrowded in the property as it only had one toilet and bathroom, so some of the bunk beds were removed. Three bedrooms would house families and one room was provided for the carer. There was a lounge with a TV and a table in the kitchen for meals. The place had an outbuilding which would have been ideal for a washroom and another toilet, but money was sparse and it would have to wait.

Interestingly, I was given a volunteer from the drug rehabilitation unit to help me. I would pick him up in the morning and he would put up curtain rails, shelves or tidy the garden. He was in his twenties and his parents had paid for him to come from England to spend six months getting off his drug habit of cocaine usage. I was told parents often sent their children abroad as it was far cheaper than rehabilitation clinics in the UK. The unit was very strict with its regime and he had to be back for 3.00 pm sessions and could not be late. I would fetch us a snack of sandwiches and ice cream from a corner shop at 12.00 noon and make us coffees and tea. We had usually had enough of jobs by 2.00 pm and would head back to the city.

Father John was very involved with the city's inter faith project. This consisted of the various religious leaders of the city promoting engagement and social action which would increase dialogue between the different faiths. They held many prayer, meditation and social events. Through this meeting, a Catholic priest heard of my volunteering at St Anne's. He asked me to visit a little orphan boy at a small Catholic home. The home was caring for some children orphaned by the unrest in Angola and Mozambique. It cared for 19 children aged between 5-17. They slept two in each bedroom and attended the local school. The orphanage had a garden, play area and small swimming pool. One boy had trapped his finger in a table and was waiting to receive some surgery on it. The home asked me if I would dress the finger, three times a week, until he could go for treatment. This I did and I had some enjoyable visits there with the group.

The housekeeper was quite strict with the children and insisted that they finish their homework before play time. Some junior boys were doing arithmetic around the times tables and were then learning spellings to put into short sentences. She knew that their only chance in life was through education.

I was invited through church to go on a prison walk! The Pollsmoor Medium Correction Centre is huge with five prisons in one. It was a cold, horrible, wet evening and there had been an accident on the motorway, so some ladies came in the car to direct me, as the prison was twelve miles from the city. About 250 people took part in the visit led by a New Orleans type jazz band. After showing our passports and going through security checks we met up in a hall and were briefed about the prison and how to pray for the prisoners and staff. We then processed along the corridors singing some hymns and shaking hands with the prisoners through the cell windows. They were very pleased to see us and have some human contact with smiling faces, as they did not get many visitors. Some asked for Bibles to be sent and others wanted a prayer said by the cell door. The cells were very crowded and I thought what a waste of young men's lives and a lot of talent. The men are locked up for years on end after getting involved with murder, rape, drugs and gangs. We saw some of the prisoners' artwork along the corridors and some other prisoners ran a bird club. Others had been given positions of responsibility such as tutoring, medical or clerical support, or as kitchen staff. I was told that some are able to make new lives with help from the churches, but the numbers incarcerated are huge.

The art and theatre scene was excellent in Cape Town. Apart from the Artscape main complex on the Foreshore, I enjoyed concerts at the Baxter Theatre and a lovely little theatre called 'The Theatre on the Bay' at Camps Bay. The Cape Town Gilbert and Sullivan Society performed 'The Gondoliers' at the Artscape which proved to be popular and packed. Another pleasure was the Chamber Music Breakfast Concerts at the

Kirstenbosch Botanical Gardens and I needed to book early as they were oversubscribed. I would be served breakfast, then enjoy the concert and afterwards I was free to explore the beautiful gardens.

John came to see me in June and we had a car tour of the Garden Route. We travelled as far as Port Elizabeth enjoying seeing the Cango Caves, the Ostrich Show Farm, the Cheetah Park, the Bartolomeu Dias museum complex at Mossel Bay and Falls River. The long journey was broken up with a night at Knysna where we enjoyed a boat ride around the lagoon. After two nights at Kariega Game Reserve, near Port Elizabeth, to see the 'big five', we flew back to Cape Town.

On one of the day trips around Cape Town we visited the large Kaylshia township, where we were shown different types of housing – most were made of wooden boarding and others built of brick. Some shacks had electricity whether legal or not, as some people just tap into the overhead wires. Residents have set up shops in container huts and we were able to visit the local witch doctor and view his many potions. There was bed and breakfast accommodation available in the township and we saw one establishment complete with a 49-inch television. We were shown a school where adults and children were studying to better themselves and various charity lodges for the destitute. One chap was selling artwork made from used Coca Cola tins and tops.

I made myself known to the St John members at their large three-storey headquarters in the Woodstock area of Cape Town and they showed me the busy eye clinic that they run there. I also saw the training rooms and they arranged for me to accompany members teaching on a four-hour First Aid update to office workers.

At the weekend I went with some members on duty to a rugby match. As the locals are very poor, they did not have transport so the St John minibus took them to their duties. Later on, one of the Cadet groups was holding a tea party for friends and supporters, trying to raise money for the coach to take them to the National Finals First Aid Competitions to be held in Port Elizabeth so I attended a lovely Sunday afternoon tea. Incidentally, the place for excellent afternoon tea was Mount Nelson Hotel, an old colonial hotel in the city centre where someone would be playing the grand piano during the afternoon.

St John was providing some basic health care cover in the townships and a home-based care course to families. I was able to see this in action on two half days, especially in the Betty's Bay Area where a care course was being held. Whilst I was in Cape Town the South African President, Thabo Mbeki, was installed as a Knight of St John in St George's Cathedral by HRH The Duke of Gloucester, but I was only able to read of it in the newspaper!

Marcia, the St John secretary, invited me to her relative's support group. Her mother-in-law lived with the family and support groups for various disabilities were just getting started. It was held in the lounge of a nursing home that look after people with dementia. I tried to give some ideas on management as Marcia's mother- in-law was getting more difficult to care for. Another group I visited was St Luke's Hospice at Newlands, another suburb of Cape Town. The manager was a St John member years ago and gave me a tour of the building. It provided day care and activities such as crafts and gardening and had provision for relatives to use when they had come long distances.

I had a couple of visits to Robben Island and each time an ex-prisoner would be our guide to explain what life was like. Even before it became a prison it had been used as a lepers' colony, to isolate them from people on the mainland. Another fact was that the Anglican Church years ago had a hostel along the waterfront for women and children going to visit their husbands who were prisoners on the island. They would have travelled many miles and were only allowed to visit twice a year. They stayed at the hostel until the tide was right for the journey across to the island and on their return, before travelling home.

The wonderful days out around the Cape will always be remembered, e.g. wine tasting at Stellenbosch, whale watching at Hermanus, the South African penguins at Boulders, Cecil Rhodes' cottage and the fishing port of Hout Bay where I enjoyed a boat trip to see the seals sunbathing on the rocks at Seal Island. Stephen came to see me and we spent a lovely week visiting the winelands at Robertson and the spa resort at Montague Springs. We also enjoyed a three-day stay at Fairy Glen, a small animal park outside Cape Town to see the elephants, zebras, lions and giraffes.

September arrived, the start of the South African spring, and I was given the chance to join a small group travelling in a minibus to visit Namaqualand on the west coast to view the amazing variety of wild flowers that grow in the area. I shared a room with an elderly lady and the guide telephoned ahead to find out where the sun was shining, so that we could witness the flowers opening at their best.

Just before I was due to fly home, St Anne's held their Annual General Meeting in the garden of the Ruyterach bungalow so that the house could be officially opened. It was the 103rd AGM on 20th September 2007. On a bright sunny afternoon, everyone was seated outside in the yard and the speeches took place. Afterwards, Father John and Elizabeth Peterson cut the ribbon across the front door with the scissors that I had been tasked to look after and everyone processed through the house to admire what had been achieved. The children gave a percussion and drum display in the garden at the back of the house and we all enjoyed refreshments in the front garden. I was thanked for my work and presented with a souvenir mug and glowing reference.

Rentia and Tony took me to the airport for the flight home and I was very sad to leave.

Footnote

Father John retired on his 65th birthday in April 2013, after 35 years in the ministry, of which 18 were at St Mark's Church. Sadly, he died in his sleep on 4th July 2013 and was called home. People of all faiths in Cape Town mourned a great man.

Chapter 25
Exploits in Penang

Selamat Datang (Peace and Welcome). My second placement as an EEPS student was to Penang, Malaysia. When on holiday visiting my son, who was teaching there, I had come across St Nicholas Home for the Blind, which was a Christian Home supported by the Anglican Church and they welcomed volunteers. Their motto from the Bible was, 'Led by faith not sight'. This home had been started by the missionaries in the 1920s and had moved to Jalan Bagan Jemal, Penang, from Singapore and Malacca, when the Philanthropist Lord Nuffield gave them the six-acre site in 1938 to develop training for blind children. The home accommodated around fifty residents and supported another fifty day-students at the school, with some teachers going out to rural areas to help isolated, disabled, children. Talking books and tapes were sent all around Malaysia from the home, as it served as the regional headquarters for the blind. They kept in close contact with the UK Torch group and RNIB groups.

My mission was to care for and support the twelve senior citizens who lived permanently in the home. They had been looked after by the missionaries years ago and could speak and understand English, and after leading useful lives they had been given sanctuary to spend their last days at the home. Their ages ranged from 65 to 88 years. They were mostly self-caring, apart from two elderly ladies who had a care assistant to help them. My main duty was to provide quizzes and music, and health care sessions, and accompany them to the hospital for check-ups. I

My seniors group, St Nicholas Home, Penang, 2010

would take them on outings in the home's minibus and generally befriend them. I had hoped to be able to undertake some care teaching sessions for the staff but at that time training did not have much priority. This went in my report and when I visited again four years later a training instructor had been appointed and retention of staff had been improved. I did manage to undertake two four-hour First Aid courses and certificates were presented to the staff at the Monday morning assembly.

Later, when I had become more well known, The King George Vth Jubilee Home for the elderly, further over the island, wanted to use my services. They asked me to provide training sessions and give some advice on the care of some of the chronically ill, e.g. stroke care. They wanted to start some day care and I gave them write-ups on how to do this, drawing on my experience of starting day clubs. They didn't pay me but gave me lovely meals and provided transport to and from home.

The 200-bedded home had independent living, sheltered care, residential and nursing care and their equipment was very good.

Blind and partially sighted teenagers stayed at the home for at least six months to gain some life skills which would enable them to find work. The departments included the wellness centre, a spa to learn reflexology and massage, the IT department for computer studies, a wicker and basketry workshop and a small bakery. Younger children came on a daily basis to be taught by skilled teachers for the blind (some were also hard of hearing), and they had three classrooms and an outside play area. The front office was the epicentre from where everything was organised. Regular postings and leaflet drops asking for donations would be conducted at the start of all the main religious festivals.

I was given a small guest room on the first floor at the back of the home. Visiting guests and clerics would use the rooms, but it was quite quiet away from the noisy teenagers' section. The room had two single beds, a desk and chair, and fitted wardrobe with cupboards. It had a shower, washbasin and toilet attached, but the main item was new air conditioning. Linen was provided by the home, but I only needed a bottom sheet, pillow and pillowcase – I used a large bath towel for a covering as it was too humid for sheets. The night lights of the home would shine through my thin curtains, so at night I wore my face shield and ear plugs.

Along the corridor was a kitchen, with a fridge and microwave, equipped with crockery and cutlery. Not much cooking was done as people mainly ate out as meals were so cheap. I would have a snack morning and evening, and tended to purchase a meal at the shopping centre. Next to the kitchen was a sitting room where after a week or so I managed to hire a television for the evenings, but the room only had a fan in it. I enjoyed the interesting programmes, e.g. endangered species including the Malaysian Tiger, programmes on Indonesia (which has the most earthquakes), Kuala Lumpur (which has the highest rate of lightning), and programmes about Vietnam, Korea and Australia.

I tried the food in the dining room, but again the food is so different that I preferred to get my own meals. I did manage to improve the hygiene in the dining room and washing up areas, and another idea that I had was to paint all the rails around the buildings the lemon-yellow colour that partially sighted people can see. This we take for granted on buses and trains in the UK, but it helped there, especially with new residents. The director held some meetings for volunteers to the home so I suggested a visitors' and volunteers' sign-in book at reception so the office knew exactly who was about and where. This led me on to fire training. There was no fire procedure and I suggested that the playing field at the back of the home would be a good area to congregate in case of fire and new large fire notices were erected.

One of the members of the Board of Directors was David Osman, an expat who spent his working life in banking, working with the HSBC. He very early on gave me a list of westernised restaurants to visit for meals and invited me to his expat lunch on St George's Day, which was very pleasant. His Lions Club held a huge fundraising event for the home called 'Walk for Sight' and I was able to help with that day.

Services were held in the home's chapel, which I attended on Friday mornings. Peter, a blind man, played the organ for the services and at the big service there on a Saturday. The first Bible in Malaysia was translated and used in Penang and there are now some 200 churches in the region. Often the seniors would run the service as they had special braille books for the prayers and readings and braille hymn books. Visiting priests and speakers came to the services and sometimes the Bishop of Penang would attend. Coffee and biscuits were served after the service, which was good for networking.

The home had a room at the back which served as a small mosque. Most of the young adults were Muslim and had their own prayer mats. There was an outdoor swimming pool around the courtyard, but this had fallen out of fashion as the students wanted to remain covered because of their religion, so I was one of the main users of the pool and enjoyed a daily swim. Later, when I returned, it had been filled in – what a shame!

Life again settled into a routine. Three mornings a week a volunteer came to do exercises with the seniors at 8.30, which I did with them. Three times a week I would do quizzes, read a story, play pop tunes of the '50s '60s and '70s, and lead discussions. This was with care assistant Sarawathy and a volunteer. We would hold tea parties for special days or birthdays. Later on, I was able to organise trips to the botanical gardens, spice garden, swimming club, the Eco Park, Batu Feringgi beach and the shopping mall.

Eco Park Picnic

Some mornings I would accompany one of the seniors to the state hospital for a check-up, as three of them were diabetic. They presented special ID cards and were seen quite quickly by a junior doctor, and if he needed more advice a consultant would enter from the next room. They did not have the GP system as in the UK and so many of the wealthier residents go to private hospitals.

Most of the seniors' week was spent doing their own washing in the laundry room, self-care, or working in the office to help with packing or mail shots. They enjoyed listening to the BBC World Service and had special wristwatches to tell the time.

The Chinese New Year of the Tiger, in February, was a very special time. Around the shopping malls and hotels many groups of young men would perform the Lion Dance. The two men under the yellow and gold costume would perform acrobatics by jumping on stands for the crowds, sometimes with Chinese music being played. The home had its own team and I watched them rehearse on the front lawn, which must have been much harder as the students had very poor sight. The music was mostly percussion of drums and cymbals.

During this time the seniors received many invitations to Chinese celebrations and I was able to accompany them. I would help fetch their meals or go up to receive dry goods on behalf of the home, e.g. bags of rice, flour, sugar and tea. At one ceremony we all received red envelopes with money in for gifts, as was their custom.

Whilst at the home two new volunteers appeared, Tom and his wife. He was a retired school caretaker and offered to paint the elderly men's dormitory where six seniors slept. I helped them clear the room and used money sent from my church to purchase six bedside cupboards so that the men could put their radios on them. The maintenance department bought them at cost price and the laundry department issued some new bottom sheets and pillows, so this was a worthwhile little project.

Valerie in Chinese

Helping in the choir at St George's Church

I purchased a little silver Kansil car (Perodua autobinee 660) as they drive on the left in Penang, so would go exploring on Saturdays to different parts of the island. The pattern on Sundays was St George's Church in the morning followed by a ride to Batu Feringgi for lunch in one of the hotels along the front. At that time St George's was closed for renovation and we used the hall for services. The choir mistress had worked at St Nicholas Home years ago and was on the board of the home. I joined the choir as they just had a quick practice for the following week after the Sunday service, which I didn't mind.

Hotels didn't mind people using the pool if visitors purchased food. This would be at the Holiday Inn, Park Royal or Hard Rock Hotel etc. I also loved to use the pool at the flats where Matthew's friends were, so Helen Teese (a teacher) would let me have her details for this.

The International Women's Association (IWA) was a club for professional women that was very active in Georgetown. I joined the group and enjoyed many visits and socials. I went to charity bazaars and book signings in hotels; one in particular was by a Chinese author who had been a health visitor for many years. I witnessed the opening of new stores and wine bars, a visit to a jewellery factory and various Christmas displays. Burns Night and St Patrick's Day were all good celebrations.

Michelle Grimsley, an ex-member, also arranged interesting visits and I went with her group on a day trip to Kuala Lumpur and to the island of Langkawi for a swim and spa day. Many day trips could be organised from the airport. Another visit on offer was with the Penang Heritage Trust to have a guided tour of the restored buildings of Georgetown; this became a UNESCO World Heritage Site in 2008 because of its eclectic buildings and character. One street is especially fascinating, 'the street of harmony', which includes temples, churches, a mosque, shrines, a heritage centre and museum. People here can learn about the peaceful co-existence of different cultures and faiths.

Indians, Chinese, Indonesians, Euro Asians and expats all make up the rich flavour of the island. Malaysia's 28 million inhabitants have a very strict government, no alcohol for Muslims and people dealing in drugs can be hanged; but the healthcare and schools were excellent. I found that mental health groups were just starting and that many of the churches in the area sent goods to clinics in neighbouring Myanmar.

One interesting story told to us, was of the toddler in her cot who was taken out to sea by the huge wave on the Boxing Day Tsunami in 2004. Fortunately, she was swept back in as another wave progressed and her story became famous. Well-wishers sent her gifts from all over the world. Many people were rehoused by the government along that north east coast of Penang, but only in very small, box-like, high rise flats, as the people were very poor and had nothing, but it was a roof over their heads to enable them to make a new start.

I enjoyed visits to the lovely colonial hotel, the E&O (Eastern and Oriental), built by the Armenian, Sarkie Brothers in 1885. They also built the Raffles Hotel in Singapore and The Strand Hotel in Yangon. It had a large swimming pool, gift shop and restaurant which served marvellous afternoon teas. My 60th birthday was celebrated with Kathleen, Matthew's teacher friend who was a music teacher at Uplands School. She was 60 in the April, as was I in June, so we went to tea at the E&O in May. She bought me a miniature teapot made from the Royal Selangor pewter and I gave her a folding teak fruit bowl. Happy days.

Kathleen invited me to the Wawasan Open University building to see Uplands School perform the Helen Keller play, 'The Miracle Worker'. I took two of the seniors along and they enjoyed the performance from some very talented young people. A country dancing evening at the school also made a lovely social time.

The St John Headquarters was further inland and ran a Kidney Dialysis Unit in connection with the Rotary Club of Penang. The members were very active and explained that they manned a quarter of the island for the ambulance service and other agencies covering the other areas. The volunteers carried out a lot of public duties especially religious festivals and sporting events, the largest being the charity marathon over Penang Bridge from Georgetown to Butterworth. They showed me the drill hall, the care room, a library, offices, training classrooms and vehicles in the garages.

I was invited to the regional competitions to be held at the University of Malaysia during April, where I was treated as an honoured guest and shown the competitions taking place around the campus. Later at the awards ceremony I was presented with a souvenir plaque. Another time I met up with the senior St John members as they wanted more information on starting fellowship groups. They were also very interested to hear about St John in other countries.

St John Friends in Penang

Near the St John buildings was Suffolk House, built on a large pepper estate owned by Captain Francis Light, founder of the British Port Settlement of Penang. It had been fully restored with grants and sponsorship by HSBC Bank in 2007 and is thought to be the finest example of an Anglo-Indian mansion outside India. It was a wonderful place to have a special meal with friends or groups.

Further afield I spent five days in the Cameron Highlands to enjoy the fresher air and see the produce of fruit and vegetables that are exported abroad through Singapore. Huge amounts of strawberries are grown and twenty lorryloads of flowers go to Singapore each day for export. I visited the BOH tea plantation to see the latest machinery used to pluck the tea leaves from the bushes. This was the largest hill resort in Malaysia and had beautiful areas of flower and tea plantations and impressive vegetable farms. This was a welcome break from the heat and humidity of Penang.

My other short break was to the east coast, to the city of Kuala Terengganu. This was a strictly Muslim state where the Red Cross was made to become part of the Red Crescent and could not use the Red Cross emblem. (While I was away, I heard that some Islamic extremists had confiscated 300 Bibles in Borneo.) I could witness the difference from Penang, a multi-cultural liberal island. I visited the Anglican priest, Canon Charles Samuel, who held his services in a hall above some shops. He wasn't allowed to build a church, so a sympathetic Christian businessman allowed the church to have space above his shops. Most of the Christians there were Chinese from the nearby university.

One of the members of the congregation showed me around the city and took me to the Islamic Civilisation Park where I viewed replicas of 21 historic Islamic monuments found around the world, including the Alhambra Citadel in Spain and the Taj Mahal in India. Another day I explored the Terengganu State museum complex, which was huge and has a maritime museum and five traditional houses showing how they were built and explaining the history and crafts of the area. I managed to book two nights away to a nearby tropical island (Redang), so went by speedboat to a beautiful hideaway for a break that looked out to the South China Sea.

As time went on my back was deteriorating, and I had a lot of lower back pain during the spring. I had attended some of the public talks held at different private hospitals around Georgetown and heard good reports about the care at the Adventist Hospital which was just around the corner from St Nicholas Home. Its profits were ploughed back into the hospital and its motto was, 'We Care and God Heals'. Michelle's mother had her gall bladder removed at the hospital and Kathleen had treatment for her heart problem there, so I decided to see a doctor in the clinic. I would have to pay, but treatment would be far cheaper than private care in the UK.

I saw the Singapore spinal surgeon, Dr Cheok Chee Yew, who ordered X-rays and said that he would give me another steroid injection like the one I had been having back home, but he thought that it wouldn't last and that I required surgery. The injection kept me pain free for only ten days and then it was back to the hospital to hear about the back operation. He explained all about it and showed me some of it from his laptop, arranging for me to have the operation at the end of the week. In the meantime, I contacted John to send the money through and went for an MRI scan, blood tests and health checks. The results were in the doctor's office before I had walked around from the diagnostic units! I was given a sarong to wear instead of a theatre gown, which proved to be quite cool.

I was in the hospital for five days, firstly in a shared room which was noisy and then in my own room. I was taken to physio each day where a tens machine was attached to stimulate the nerve cells and do exercises. I didn't like the food, so existed on sandwiches from the canteen and cartons of drinks brought in by Helen and Kathleen. On discharge I was given a CD of my results and X-rays, and the staff booked me into the hydrotherapy unit for twice weekly appointments in the new outdoor swimming pool. This had a large canopy over it, to shelter patients from the hot sun and the sessions were very effective.

I returned home in May 2010 via Cape Town where I met up with John and we stayed five days to renew visits to friends and acquaintances. John had booked the RAFA Social Club at RAF Halton to celebrate my 60th birthday in June, so I was able to meet up with my friends and catch up on all the news. I held a large raffle at the party which raised £350 for the St John Eye Hospital, which seems a fitting end to this chapter of my life.

CHAPTER 26
EXPLOITS IN MYANMAR

"I have come that they may have life and have it to the full."

John 10:10

Myanmar was an unusual placement and I never thought that I would end up there! During the autumn of 2017 a brochure was posted through the letterbox to advertise goods for Christmas from the Leprosy Mission. I had always been passionate about trying to help people suffering from leprosy – it is such an old biblical disease, though completely curable today if caught early. Multi-drug therapy has been available since the 1980s but poor

people in developing countries with fledgling health services cannot access treatment. They are afraid that they will be ostracised by their family, or lose their job, so they don't go for early diagnosis or treatment.

I wrote to the office of the Leprosy Mission at Peterborough with my CV and travel experience and was called for an interview there. I was expecting that they would send me to India, as that has the most cases in the world, but they chose Myanmar because they thought that I would be able to give teaching sessions and that I would be ideal to become one of their voluntary speakers on my return.

The main problem was getting permission for a volunteer to work there as it is still quite a closed country. Several letters were sent on my behalf and the next challenge was to gain the visa. When this was not very forthcoming, John and I went to London early one morning to be at the Myanmar Embassy at 10.00 am for the opening. They took my documents and asked me to return at 4.00 pm. We returned later and everything had been stamped approved. The Peterborough staff were amazed, as usually it takes weeks to gain approval!

I wanted to go as soon as possible as the temperature there was rising and could get to 38 degrees just before the monsoons. I had permission to stay for up to six months but in fact only stayed for ten weeks from March 2018. This was because the heat became so oppressive and John was on his own more now that he had finished work. I was spending twenty dollars a night at my boarding house opposite the hospital and that was mounting up, as the experience was completely self-funded.

I purchased three boxes of tinned goods in Yangon to take with me as I travelled down to Mawlamyine, the large town in southern Myanmar where the hospital was situated. This was a six-hour journey from Yangon, the capital. My main mentors were Dr Roma Hein, a retired public health doctor, and Matron Ni Ni Thein. I travelled from Yangon with Dr Roma and some other staff in the Leprosy Mission's estate car; she advised me to wear uniform the first few days so that the staff could get to know me. Dr Roma organised some breakfast to be delivered to the guest house to get me started and I managed to find a taxi driver who spoke English that I could call on my mobile phone for lifts to the supermarket.

The guest room only had a fridge and kettle so meals were limited. Matron gave me some utensils and a toaster and occasionally I would have a meal in the shopping centre. The local food was watery boiled rice, curries, sugary desserts and other dishes that I could not manage. The bedroom had no wardrobes or cupboards, as is the custom there, so most of my belongings stayed in the suitcase and boxes. The television had one English-speaking channel which was broadcast from Germany. It was a magazine-type channel with regular news updates. One very good programme was at Easter about Cologne Cathedral.

On the first day Matron showed me around the hospital and gave me a power point presentation on Leprosy. The main hospital buildings were in poor condition, some having been built as prefabs by supporters from the Netherlands in the 1990s. The outpatients building was new with air conditioning and had been donated by the States of Jersey. The only ward with air conditioning was the Reaction Ward where the most severely affected patients were nursed – they could stay for up to a year for treatment. Many were nursed on old wooden beds with only a thin mattress and no pillow or sheets. Matron had been able to purchase ten newer beds but bedding was in short supply. Relatives came with the patients and brought them food and helped care for them.

The central nurses' station in the middle of the building was where the staff could supervise and delegate the nursing. There were only four trained nurses in the hospital so it relied heavily on the senior nursing assistants. Some patients had the added

Matron with dressing assistant

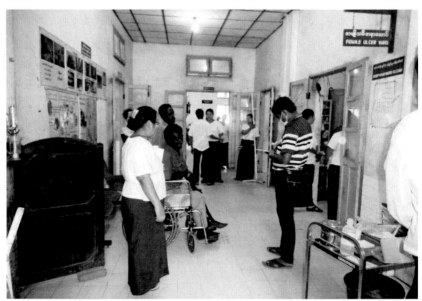

Outside the dressing room

complications of malnutrition, diabetes, heart or kidney failure, fever, ulcers and pain. Large doses of steroids were used to help the severe cases and much research worldwide is going on to find more effective drugs, more treatments for leg ulcers and a vaccine.

In another building 30 nursing assistants were attending a six-month course to gain a recognised Health Care Assistant's Certificate. They were given three months theory and three months practical. Their relatives had saved money so that the girls could attend, as this would enable them to get a job in hospitals and clinics in other parts of the country – they stayed in a hostel down the road from the hospital. An older girl called Angela was a Catholic nun and could understand and speak English, so she was a great help to translate for me during the training sessions. This training scheme also brought a little money to the hospital and was good for morale. The subjects I

Training sessions with the care assistants

covered included, Infection Control, Hygiene, Nutrition, Strokes, Health and Safety, First Aid, Tuberculosis and Moving and Handling, which is what they asked for and I was fortunate to be able to use the handouts that I took, which helped a great deal. I tried to show them some modern teaching ways such as quizzes, seminars, discussions and practical work, as their teaching was still very much talk and chalk and copying from the screen or text papers.

And so a routine developed. I attended the doctors' round each morning at 9.30 when they would look at the wounds and prescribe the treatments to be carried out or see how cases were progressing. On the ward rounds were two physiotherapists who explained what was happening and were able to speak English, and I would then go with them to observe the sessions in the Rehabilitation Unit. Some patients were given traction, exercises, tens machine electrical impulses and laser treatment to help stimulate the damaged nerves. The other physio would often need to make Plaster of Paris splints to rest limbs, which would enable the wounds to heal.

One morning I was able to observe the operations taking place in the operating theatre to see damaged tendons in the fingers and hands being released, so that patients could use their hands again. Only spinal and local anaesthetics were given as they didn't have an anaesthetist. Next-door was a dressing room where staff cut the dressings to size and used the autoclave to sterilise the dressings and equipment. They did not have the luxury of dressing packs. Late morning, I would go to the dressings clinic which was situated just off the wards – here patients would come every other day to have their dressings changed. It was cleaned very well each day and staff had separate shoes to wear there, but it badly required new sealed windows and air conditioning. Yaw, the dressing nurse, was very efficient and good at his job. He had empathy and commitment and showed other staff how to perform some difficult desloughing procedures.

Two nuns in the physio department

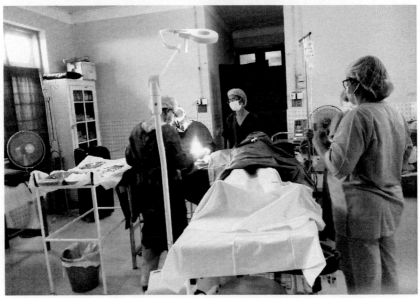

Repairing damaged ligaments in theatre

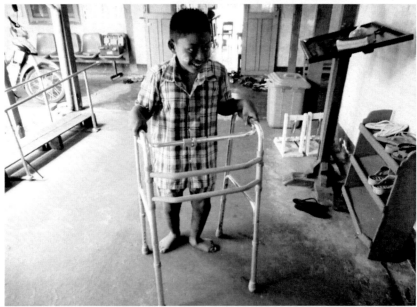

Disabled children arriving for day care

Each morning a pick-up van (a sortal) would arrive with several disabled children, who would spend the day in the day care room whilst their parents were at work. Some children had cerebral palsy, others were autistic or epileptic. They were taught basic reading and writing and enjoyed craftwork and music. This helped the hospital earn money. Some children wore Taneka powder (from the wood apple tree) on their cheeks to protect the skin from the blazing sun, others wore it as make up, to make them look pretty.

The people were very poor, and I witnessed the Save the Children, World Vision, the Red Cross, UNICEF and the World Food Bank vans in operation when I went for walks around the town. The dust cart came along outside the hospital every morning playing a tune and this was my alarm to go over to the hospital and start work.

I carried out three sessions per week to each of the three groups and other days I went into the town to explore. The teaching sessions tended to take place during the afternoons when most of the work had been completed. I was giving sessions to the ward staff in the nurses' station at 1.00 pm and sessions in the teaching room for the care assistants. At 4.00 pm I managed to hold English speaking lessons for some of the younger staff who wanted to learn conversational English. These were held in the physiotherapist's office as he had air conditioning and would arrange for someone to bring me tea or a cold drink! Some days, I was able to sit in the consulting room in the new outpatients clinic and observe the doctor looking at the skin diseases.

Because of the heat, dirt, poor diet and flies, the hospital saw an assortment of conditions such as Impetigo, Ringworm, Scabies, Fungal infections, Eczema and insect bites, as well as the tell-tale Leprosy patches. The doctor would shine a torch on the skin and could tell what the problem was. There was a small path lab for blood tests and a pharmacy where the patients could purchase their tablets and creams. Other issues were people with foot drop, loss of sensation in the hands or feet, eye damage and hair loss.

Off-duty I managed to find two hotels with swimming pools where I could pay to use the facilities. I also enjoyed three lovely trips. Matron took me with her sister-in-law south of Mawlamyine, where we visited an HIV/Aids clinic run by nuns, where we had a rest by the coast and I was able to have a swim. She also showed me one of the early first Baptist Churches that was built by the missionaries who came over from America between 1700-1826. We visited the Burma Death Railway and War Commission Graves, as I had seen the other end of the railway at Kanchanaburi in Thailand.

The second trip was to Ogre Island just across the estuary. An enterprising Buddhist hotel owner took visitors across on a day trip. He managed to find five other visitors who were young back packers, so off we set in a small boat. On the other side he had a minibus waiting that took us to see how slate was made to produce blackboards for schools and how coconut mats were woven for mats in homes and monasteries. The next stop was to watch dyed rubber being sliced to make elastic bands, after which we went to the island's outdoor pool where we were ready for a dip and to freshen up. He took us to a local café for a two-course lunch, and then it was more visits to a coconut plantation to hear how the coconut oil is collected every evening – it takes twenty pots to make one rubber mat. Our last visits were to see reed sun hats being made and to a souvenir stall. The island has 250,000 inhabitants and still makes a lot of the craft items for Burma. We were driven back from the island over the new bridge which the locals were proud of.

The last outing was with the student nursing assistants to see the huge limestone caves in the hills at the back of the town. These are a haven for wildlife, especially seven different species of bats! Unfortunately, the caves had become Buddhist shrines so to walk through we were expected to remove our shoes. It was not very pleasant walking on the rough gravel floor, but the girls seemed to enjoy the experience. Matron was wise and stayed by the coach. Each town and village we came to expected a tip or safety money to pass through – this earned the area money, but when they saw it was the Leprosy transport, it was often refused.

Myanmar should be a rich country as it has very good natural resources of oil, gems (rubies and jade), teak forests, rice, rubber, spices and fruit, but since 1962 it has been ruled by a Military Junta that has seen corruption and mismanagement; also, many ethnic groups fight each other and destabilise the country. After Aung San Suu Kyi's National League of Democracy won the election in 2010 things improved a little and the country started to open up to tourism, but the reforms were short lived and many of the old ways continued. The Internet did not get established until 2015 and the currency is so worthless that foreigners are required to pay in American dollars. I had to go to a special bank in town to change money each week from the local Kyats to American dollars in order to pay the guest house.

When I was leaving, a special tea time ceremony was held in the hall and I was presented with some small gifts. The English students gave me a set of towels, Angela gave me a small crocheted shawl and Matron a cloth bag. Dr Roma gave me some material for a sarong. I was able to present to the Medical Superintendent with £900 from my church and fundraising to encourage them to have some decorating and maintenance carried out. I also bought some new mops and buckets after my hygiene sessions. Feedback since my visit has reported that a deep clean was carried out and decorating done. This year, 2020, it was the Leprosy Mission's project to raise money for the Myanmar hospital, but the Covid 19 outbreak will have spoiled this much needed fundraising effort.

Dr Roma insisted on travelling back to Yangon with me on the Greyhound-type coach. She seemed worried that I would get left behind at the rest stop as I didn't understand the language. She spent most of the journey chewing betel nuts which made her lips red. At the highway café, we saw some monks whom she said must have their food eaten before 12.00 noon. Sure enough, a bell was sounded at 12 o'clock and the food was finished.

Luckily, I had found a small boutique hotel near the centre of Yangon and spent some days exploring the city. It was colonised by the British years ago and was administered by them from India – the capital was then called Rangoon. Independence came in 1948 but democracy was short lived when the military Junta came to power in 1962.

I was able to visit the wonderful Swedagon Pagoda that stands 325 feet high and has 2,317 rubies and 5,448 diamonds around it. There were golden temples in every town and village, giving it the name of 'The Land of the Golden Pagodas'. I managed to visit the National Zoo that badly required new enclosures, and the Drug Education Museum, as Myanmar is the second largest producer of opium in the world. One morning I went to the famous five-star Strand Hotel. It had a lot of character, and in the foyer I watched a man play the Saung-gaug, a type of boat-shaped harp that has 13 strings. Noel Coward, Somerset Maughan, George Orwell and Rudyard Kipling had all stayed there, and like Raffle's Hotel in Singapore it oozes old world charm.

U Thant's house was open to the public on certain days and I was able to look around and see photographs of him when he was Secretary General of the United Nations (1961-1971), meeting Kennedy, Khrushchev and many famous people including John Lennon. The large house is now used for events and lectures.

A new travel route for flights had recently started between Yangon and Phuket, Thailand, so I was able to fly direct and meet up with my son, Matthew, for some rest and relaxation.

Visiting the Swedagon Pagoda and Temples, Yangon

Total Bliss! Hotel Royale, Phuket

Here is a copy of the email I received a few months afterwards to say that the work was done and the place had been improved!

> *Dear Valerie,*
>
> *I had a very good visit to MCLH with a visitor GP who was actually very impressed with the hospital – I wasn't told that by previous visitors, so this is a sign things have changed there, in itself! Actually, it is five years since I visited MCLH – last time I found it all shabby, a bit uncared for, not so clean. But this time it was very bright, newly painted (photos attached), some parts of the hospital had been refurbished, everywhere was squeaky clean, there was new equipment looking well cared for, and patients seemed more upbeat. Really it was like chalk and cheese – I really wondered if I was visiting the same place.*
>
> *I think you have had a wonderful influence on the place in terms of its cleanliness and professionalism and people seem to be taking more pride in the place. From your funds the repainting had been done inside and out (I forgot to ask about all the other bits).*
>
> *Dr Roma has also had a great role and there are some changes in attitudes – the guest house and the role of the board are changing too. I think your visit served to reinforce what she, as well as the nurse/staff who visited from Bangladesh and Nepal, had been saying to move things forward. I feel MCLH is now very much moving in the right direction.*
>
> *Thank you for your time and input in helping to make this happen.*
>
> *Warm regards*
>
> *James Pender*
>
> *Programmes & Advocacy Officer – Asia*
>
> *The Christian Leprosy Mission.*

CONCLUSION

Recounting these memoirs has helped me to appreciate what an interesting and meaningful life I have led. Probably the most stressful time was the last few years of my career working at the John Hampden Unit at Stoke Mandeville Hospital. This was because the job was rapidly changing and resources were reduced, so the managers wanted the staff to work in different ways. Out went the community work and taking referrals from the General Practitioners' Health Centre meetings. Referrals would be direct to the Mental Health Team and be allocated to the most appropriate professional. Staff would just go out to visit and assess one isolated client, not know anything about other elderly patients in the area. Day clubs were started and run through Social Services, not receiving practical support from the CPNs. Charities, such as Age UK, Carers Bucks and the Alzheimer's Society ran support groups, respite care and training. Early proactive work was discouraged and the work became very prescriptive and less varied. I had loved the more 'personal', practical aspects in earlier years, but all this had now changed.

Fortunately, I had enough years of service to be able to step down on reaching my 55th birthday. I was able to access my Health Service pension and I was still young enough to try some new challenges. I ran the day clubs for a few years, then managed to have several wonderful placements abroad, until John felt ready to retire when he was 65. These were the most adventurous and exciting times of my life. It was such a privilege to be able experience different cultures and settings, and to be part of life there, where I could use my initiative. It was so much better to be working and engaging as part of a team and so different from being a tourist, just briefly skimming the surface of a place. These travels made me realise how lucky and blessed I have been.

POSTSCRIPT

John and I have now lived in Christchurch for six years now and really love the area. We joined several groups and made friends with a variety of people. Every year friends and family from Aylesbury and beyond come to stay for bed and breakfast, and we tend to visit Aylesbury and stay with Linda and Paul in the spring and autumn to catch up.

Steve has a partner Emma and a son called Arthur William, born on 1st June 2020, and they have a house in Biggleswade. Steve is

With Steve, Emma and Arthur

Travels with Matt

a fire fighter at Bedford Fire Station and Emma is a nurse at Stevenage Hospital. Matthew continues with his teaching at international schools and has recently taught in Athens.

Life has been very good with lots of days out and travel. Let us hope that we can resume our normal life after the world has used the vaccine.

Thanks for making it to the end. If you have enjoyed reading this book it half as much as I have enjoyed writing it, then it's been worth all the effort.

Valerie

January 2021

Please recommend this book to your friends and associates to purchase, as the proceeds are for the St John Eye Hospital, Jerusalem.

theyoungteam2001@hotmail.com

With Hazel and Dot on my 70th birthday, June 2020